Place

Space

Markku Hakuri

(ed.)

PLACE OF SPACE

Aalto University publication series
Art+Design+Architecture 6/2014

School of Arts, Design and Architecture
Aalto ARTS Books
Helsinki, Finland
books.aalto.fi

ISBN 978-952-60-5673-9
ISSN-L 1799-4853
ISSN 1799-4853
ISSN 1799-4861 [pdf]

© The authors and Aalto University

Photos by Markku Hakuri
unless stated otherwise
Graphic design: Anne Pasanen
Photo Editor: Kaarina Hakuri
Publishing Editor: Sanna Tyyri-Pohjonen
Translation: Esa Lehtinen

This book has been produced in
cooperation with Helsingin Energia.

Typeface: Progress Two,
Plantin Std, Simplon BP Mono
Materials: Munken Pure 120G, MaxiSilk 150G,
Curious Matter Black Truffel 380G

Printed by Aldus
Lahti, Finland 2014

PAIKKA

JAN-ERIK ANDERSSON (b. 1954) is a Finnish artist whose works are dealing with primary biological, psychological and sociological energies of being human – loving, constructing, communicating, eating, dreaming, playing. Since 1980 he has presented installations, performances, public art works, interactive media works and architecture. Since 1991 he has been a member of the performance group Edible Finns. Andersson's best known work is the total artwork Life on a Leaf, where he lives with his family. The house, a product of collaboration with architect Pitkäranta, was the subject for his Doctorate in Visual Arts 2008 at the Academy of Fine Arts in Helsinki. The project explores the house as a membrane between nature and culture and the potential of art and ornamentation to create iconic space. www.anderssonart.com

VAI

POLLY BALITRO (b.1987) is an Italian art photographer with a Master in Environmental Art, currently based in Helsinki, Finland. Interested in analogue image making, travelling, culture and history and especially inspired by the natural environment, her works are mainly photographic series, though some of them go beyond the mere two-dimensional image: these multilayered projects are forms of installations through which she tries to interact with her audience. www.pollybalitro.com

SCOTT ELLIOTT (b.1979) is a Canadian installation artist, teacher, graduate of the Environmental Art MA program of Aalto University and PhD candidate at RMIT University. Constantly searching for new understanding of our ways of being in the world, through art, research, and writing. www.scottandrewelliott.com

TILA

MARKKU HAKURI (b.1946) is a Finnish visual artist. Since 1976, he has been exhibiting regularly at solo exhibitions and participating in a great number of group exhibitions. Hakuri has taught at many Finnish institutions of higher education and has worked as a visiting teacher at many foreign universities. Between 2000 and 2012, he worked as Professor for Environmental Art at the University of Art and Design Helsinki, later Aalto University. In addition to his active career as an artist and teacher, Hakuri has worked as a set and visual designer. For Hakuri, to make art is to experiment and to take conscious risks. He sees art as constituting the lexicon of our being-in-the-world, the content of which is determined at the critical juncture between imagination and knowledge. www.markkuhakuri.eu

TRISTAN HAMEL (b. 1983) is a French visual artist based in Finland. He holds several degrees from French and Finnish universities. As an artist, he exhibited in Finland, Germany and the USA. His practice consists of both indoors and outdoors works. Often based or being part of expeditions in the natural environment, Hamel's work intends to explore and reveal some aspects of the relationship people foster with the place they live in, with a particular focus on sociocultural aspects. More recently, Hamel developed an interest in the role of technology in the aesthetic appreciation of nature. www.tristanhamel.eu

MARTTI HYVÖNEN was born in 1947 in Helsinki, Finland. He studied medicine in Montpellier, France, and specialized in Occupational Medicine and General Practice. Having worked since 1974 as Chief Physician in the industry he became Environmental Director at Helsinki Energy in 2001. He retired in the beginning of 2014. His fields of expertise have been air pollution and health, asbestos, energy efficiency and the electromagnetic field issues. Risk communication and interaction with various stakeholders are areas of special interest for him. He has been Chairman of environmental working groups in Finland and within Eurelectric in Brussels. In the cultural field, Martti Hyvönen is interested in languages, the Renaissance, and conceptual and environmental art. His favourite sports are cycling and boxing. He is engaged in Finnish-French associations and the Society of philosophy in medicine.

PLACE

OR

SPACE

OSSI NAUKKARINEN (b. 1965), PhD, Vice Dean, Head of Research at the Aalto University School of Arts, Design and Architecture, and docent in aesthetics at the University of Helsinki. He has the responsibility for education planning at the Aalto ARTS since 2012. Naukkarinen also teaches and does research. He is particularly interested in what is known as everyday aesthetics. He wants to lead a full life that is not all work. Family, friends, sports and outdoor activities, travel, music, books, exhibitions and good food are just as important to him.

DAN SNOW (b.1951) is an artist specializing in dry stone constructed, environmental art commissions. Author of two books on stone-work, Dan is a Pratt Institute alumnus and a Mastercraftsman with the Dry Stone Walling Association of Great Britain. Snow has instructed stone craft, lectured on art and design, and built site specific sculpture in Northern Europe and across North America. He lives in his native state of Vermont, USA. The craft of dry stone is problem-solving. The art of dry stone is the creation of new problems to solve. Art making outdoors with natural materials connects us to our original expressive impulses as human beings and leads us toward a fuller understanding of ourselves and our world. www.dansnowstoneworks.com

LAURA UIMONEN (b.1969) is a Finnish multi-talent in the field of art. After graduating as an architect, Uimonen first became a regional artist, and undertook projects and further studies to become an art researcher. Since 2007, she has worked as the executive director of the Voipaala art centre. Her dissertation about the pairing of public art and urban planning was completed in 2010, and she continued with the same themes in a percentage for art report in 2013. The thread that runs through her work is the environment: its planning, the related phenomena, and the opportunities that artists have to participate in the debate on the environment. She also feels that the many ways in which we experience our environment are equally part of both urban planning and art.

KURT VANBELLEGHEM (b.1968) is a Belgian curator and publisher of contemporary art and design. He received a Master's in Psychological sciences and in Art History at the University of Ghent, Belgium and in Visual Arts Administration at the Royal College of Art, London, UK. He is specialized in current art & design practices and theories. His focus is on creating a synergy between both disciplines in regards to their relevance towards the society. He has been a contributing editor to a number of art & design magazines and has published several monographs and artist's books. Since 2010 he also works as a curator at St Lucas University College of Art & Design in Antwerp Belgium, where he coordinates extra-curriculum projects for students and alumni.

JAN KENNETH WECKMAN (b.1946), artist, born in, Helsinki, works in Turku and lives in Rusko. He works with drawing, painting and digital printmaking and has exhibited his works in Finland and abroad since 1969. In 2005 Weckman graduated from the Fine Art Academy, Helsinki. His doctoral thesis work focused on a semiotic approach in discussing artistic practice. Weckman has had a long career as an art teacher mainly at the former University of Art and Design (now Aalto University). He has engaged himself, besides artworks, in thesis evaluation and writing about art related topics. The interests picked up from the thesis work draws a route around art as communication. www.jankennethweckman.fi

PLACE

OR

SPACE

Tampere 37 km
Rooma 2278 km

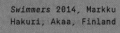

Swimmers 2014, Markku
Hakuri, Akaa, Finland

Place or Space

Markku
Hakuri

Place or Space

And how about our most beautiful creations – architecture, art, and the many manifestations of our spirit? Will any of them stand the test of time, or at least until the time when the Sun eventually expands and scorches the Earth?

— Alan Weisman, *The World Without Us,* 2008:15

The creation of this book was inspired by environmental art, an art form that potentially brings together responsibility and freedom; claiming public spaces; a discussion of the environment in terms of visual forms and values; temporary or permanent works of art; and the importance and meaningfulness of people's environmental actions.

The book is a collection of articles, the authors of which are my colleagues, cooperation partners and recent Aalto University graduates. The book tells the story of places and spaces that we, the authors, encountered when reflecting on the potential of art as a provider of social commentary, and a shaper and challenger of the visual appearance of our environment. To us, environmental art has primarily meant acts, the motivation for which lies in aesthetic, ethical and environmental issues and reflections.

In 2001, a professorship of environmental art was established at the University of Art and Design Helsinki by a donation from the Tuusula municipality. I held this position from 2001 to 2012. The international degree programme in environmental art was established in 2004. In 2010, the University of Art and Design Helsinki merged into the Aalto University. Along with the degree reforms at the university, the degree programme in environmental art will end in its current form at the beginning of August in 2014. My twelve years of working within environmental art education provide the framework for this book.

The book discusses environmental art and its contents, while shedding light on the challenges in environmental art education and practices. The intention is to demonstrate the great range of opportunities and the wide application of environmental art in the field of art, as the various authors clarify those aspects of the environment and art that were explored in the degree programme.

In the context of environmental art, place and space are easily interpreted as synonyms. Both words are used to describe, for example, a bounded space, the characteristics of which are defined by the observer's interpretation and

PAIKKA

experience. In environmental art, place and space form a combination, the characterisation and dimensions of which depend on the observer's perspective and world view.

Questions of place and space are at the crux of environmental art and its teaching: place-specificity, the spirit of a place, the importance of a space and its dimensions. The examination of a place and a space grows from the details of a place to the spatial dimensions of a space. This means that a place can be an unbounded space in three-dimensional space. It can be a bounded space, area or landscape. It can be a part of a whole. It can express a situation or a particular time. Space is no less ambiguous as a concept. A space can signify locality or the extent of a place. It can refer to the location, size and boundaries of a place. In the Finnish language, a space can also refer to the state and circumstances related to an environment or a situation. The questions of place and space are always linked to the observer's cultural background.

The reflections on place and space also include a broader, more abstract dimension. A place in a spatial, unbounded space leads us to think about the fundamental questions of life, and the understanding of life as being consciousness bounded by the concepts of time and space. Our place in the world is an image created by our experiences. Our experience of the world, and of the life we have lived, has built the places of our selfhood. They can surprise us with a familiarity, a fondness or a sense of the world. We may have a realisation of the world in a place that is meaningful to us.

VA I

Understanding the significance of place, its cultural links and its subjective experience, has been one of the premises for environmental art education. Although the subjects covered in the studies, for the most part, relate to very concrete and practical questions, lying in the background is always a wider exploration into the meaning of our existence and its individual understanding. Art has the potential to reflect on these complex questions that bring together scientific truths and visions of the imagination. Art is a forge of free thought and association, in which experiences, memories and emotions provide a basis for understanding and knowledge. The channels of knowledge offered by art, emotion and empathy, are just as essential as any other approach to understanding fundamental questions. Art calls for a holistic worldview, in which everything influences everything else, and in which human actions, our stories, are part of a broader field of knowledge.

TILA

According to Oliver Sacks (Oliver Sacks, *The Man Who Mistook His Wife for a Hat*, 1998), our place in the world, our space in the universe, is based on pre-human memories and landscapes. This means information from the distant past, information that is ill-suited to supporting a rational and empirical view of the world. Sacks writes about the inner human story, the continuity and meaning of which is our life. This story is our identity, which is constantly and unconsciously being shaped by our perceptions, feelings, ideas, actions and speech. In this story, the places that we consider important are like lighthouses that help us navigate through different environments.

Experience and knowledge

Imagination is more important than knowledge
—Albert Einstein

Experience produces knowledge. In the words of Leonardo da Vinci: "Wisdom is the daughter of experience". A photograph of a garden of the Kayapó tribe, from the book *Amazonia* by Jukka Salo and Mikko Pyhälä (1991, p. 207), has left a strong imprint on my mind. At first glance, it looks like a jungle. However, the book goes on to reveal that it is a garden that mimics the rainforest. Cultivated plants are grown together so they provide each other with shelter from the sun, wind and rain. Knowing that the picture presents a garden with numerous different plant species confuses the viewer. At the same time, what we see takes on whole new dimensions. From what looks like chaos, beauty of knowledge emerges. It is knowledge about the purpose of use of the plants and the necessary conditions to cultivate them. The photograph in the book shows a Kayapó man standing in the middle of a rainforest that he has delicately organised and that provides him with everything he needs in life: food, shelter, materials, medicine, and so on. Indigenous people have, throughout history, processed and used numerous plants for food and medicine. The knowledge of indigenous people is the history of experience.

Experience, learning by doing, is a fundamental pillar of art education. It means workshops that aim at mastering the process of making art, from planning to actual implementation. Learning by doing means experimenting with materials and techniques and testing imaginative ideas and plans. Learning by doing means finding surprising combinations that allow the visible reality (the environment) and the experiencer's state of mind to, together, open up new pathways towards consciousness and understanding. Surprising combinations are based on creativity, the ability to organise and see things in a new way.

Another important fundamental in art education is offering guidance based on the student's individual world view. It is important to recognise the subjective reality and values of each student, to highlight their unique individual characteristics, and their cultural bonds and backgrounds. Even if our physical environment was the same, it would mean different things to each of us.

We interpret the visible reality through our own experience and values. This is the reason that the interaction between student and teacher, and individual student guidance, is vitally important.

The third fundamental of art education is the interaction between other art and science disciplines, and active involvement in social debate and reflection on the structures of the social environment. In practice, this is realised through sharing experience and knowledge, which enables the opening up of new perspectives. New perspectives emerge from surprising juxtapositions and unexpected encounters. We need an open mind, and the courage to interact, fail and perform seemingly futile acts.

The premises of environmental art education could be summarised as follows. Study involves learning by doing, gaining experiential knowledge, set against the background of the student's individual world view, and engaging in interaction with other arts and sciences. The aim of the studies is to encourage students to find surprising juxtapositions, to institute positive change and to unlearn which should translate into boldness of expression and freedom of thought. There is no right way to make art.

The framework of environmental art allows us to discuss issues related to our environment from a very broad perspective. The reflection on place and space, and the importance of experience and knowledge, make for prime examples. The visual appearance of our environment is not unambiguously an aesthetic issue. We will, increasingly, have to reflect on the acts that affect and change our environment. The constant change caused by human activity, including agriculture, forestry, mining, construction, and transport, is our most fundamental challenge going into the future. At stake is the future of our most precious place, the Earth.

Yhteisötaide

Community Art

Hauki / Pike 2011, Suomussalmi, Finland

Tuliseremonia / Fire Ceremony 2004, Suomussalmi, Finland

Palavat tornit / Burning Towers 2003, Savitaipale, Finland

Palavat tornit / Burning Towers 2003, Savitaipale, Finland

Toivomuskaivot / Wishing Wells 2011, Kerava Art Museum, Finland

Ketju / Chain 2003, Bengtskär, Finland

Get Wired!

Tristan
Hamel

Get Wired!

For the last twenty years, digital technologies have had a broad and deep impact on our societies. In the field of environmental art, however, the generalisation of computing or telecommunication seems to have gone largely unnoticed, which may reveal difficulties in renewing our practices and the way we look at art. This is to be regretted, since digital technologies are potentially powerful tools in the attempt to promote the inclusion of person and place as a mode of aesthetic experience. More than the lack of interest from the side of the artists, it is probable that what is in question is the difficulties of some other actors to widen their understanding of environmental art.

When examining environmental art, critics and academic writers usually consider the movement to have emerged in the 1960s. It already has a well-established track record, an observation reinforced by the existence of dedicated study programmes, the many environmental art festivals taking place every year, the number of anthologies, and the countless exhibitions intending to offer an overview of the work of environmental artists. But what is environmental art? Unlike some other movements, no final definition can be put forward. Depending on the writer, one aspect or another is favoured. Among these, we can mention the use of a very varied set of materials, location-specificity of artworks, spatiality, and reliance on documentation. These characteristics are in no way normative: some artworks do comply with them, some others don't, and yet they may be identified as environmental artwork.

The identification of a common set of characteristics is not an enterprise that scholars and critics have engaged in for the mere sake of categorisation, but with the ambition of outlining a framework within which the relative value of different artworks could be assessed. Criticisms of categorisation are customary, not least from the artists themselves, who are often reluctant to identify themselves as environmental artists, maybe because they consider the term to impose too stringent limits on their creative freedom. However, from the moment we assume that art is for appreciation, and that not all artworks are of equal worth, such categories are necessary. Indeed, when we intend to assess the value of an artwork, we do so from a comparative perspective. If we try to go beyond our intuition and specify the aesthetic characteristics of one artwork in particular, we must know with which other work we ought to compare it. Roberts Smithson's *Spiral Jetty* is not a valuable artwork as such, nor is it in comparison with *the Mona Lisa, the Magic Flute,* or *Metropolis.* It is a valuable artwork when looked at in the context of land art or environmental art, rather than in the context of the arts as a whole. Yet, the definition of environmental art remains vague, fifty years after its emergence, and there may be as many definitions as there are scholars and critics writing about it. Unlike other movements, such as Surrealism or Dadaism, there were no manifestos or grand gestures marking its birth and through which we could look at any subsequent works. For the purpose of this short article, instead of engaging in a painstaking review of the many definitions proposed during the last few decades, we will assume that appreciation of environmental art largely relies on its rejection of the traditional form of engagement with the environment, and its promotion of inclusion between person and place. Material criteria necessarily apply but, as they are not needed for the rest of our discussion, we will leave them aside.

Now we may ask ourselves how environmental art promotes the inclusion of person and place today. Do contemporary artists make use of the same tools as their predecessors? Are their practices located in similar environments? Has their social focus shifted or do they direct their attention to identical phenomena? In short, how do contemporary environmental artists fare with the weight of legacy? Or, put in yet another way, how did environmental art evolve while the society it is set in was undergoing major transformations?

To conduct a comprehensive analysis of the history of the movement goes beyond the goals of this article. Instead, we will concentrate on one aspect that is commonly accepted as a major evolution of the last 30 years, which is the boom of digital technologies, considered in a broad sense, and including computing, digital communication, and micro-electronics. It is a commonplace that the generalisation of these technologies has had significant social repercussions. Some argue that the impact was so broad, possibly touching every sphere of human life, and so deep, as it radically reshapes many of our behaviours, that the epoch we live in can be clearly distinguished from previous ones. Beyond their social aspect, the generalisation of digital technologies is also noticeable in the physical layer of our environment. As for direct effects, it has led to the building of large industrial areas such as data centres, assembling factories, mines and ore processing plants, and to the multiplication of telecommunication masts in the landscape. Indirectly, and probably more significantly, the calculation power of computers and the speed of data transfer afforded by modern telecommunications have led to a re-organisation of existing activities, and therefore to a transformation of the environments in which they are carried out. To give but one example, the intensity of air traffic nowadays could not be reached without digital technologies and, as a consequence, rare are the places on the planet where, on a sunny day, one can admire a clear blue sky empty of the typical steam trails of jet liners. In as remote areas as central Siberia, the sky is striped by the many aeroplanes linking Europe to Asia. Lastly, digital technologies have had a significant impact on a macro level, for instance as a significant demographic factor. Digital hubs offering extended connectivity are nowadays attractive areas where the population is growing and where economic dynamism induces an intense building effort and a rapid urbanisation of the environment. In contrast, regions once prosperous and attractive, for instance because of the abundance of natural resources, are depopulating, with brownfield sites replacing factories and sometimes giving way to a return to wilderness. Naturally, it is unlikely that these geographical transformations are caused solely by the rise of digital technologies. Yet, among the multiple reasons proposed by geographers, our passage into the "information age" does play its role.

In this context, it is legitimate to enquire about the changes in environmental art practice. The question touches upon at least two aspects of the art practice, distinct from one another: the use of digital technologies as tools and as subject matter.

Firstly, it is quite clear that digital technologies have not become an ordinary part of the environmental artist's toolbox. No comprehensive survey has been conducted to reach this conclusion, but anyone browsing websites dedicated to the field or visiting exhibitions revolving around it will easily notice that artists are not particularly taking advantage of the possibilities offered by digital technologies. This is also the case with the documentation of artworks, rarely drifting out of traditional forms such as photography or films. One could counter-argue that digital technologies are, in fact, used by artists as much as they are by any other professional, would this not directly reflect in the art work. Indeed, artists would often do background research on the Internet, examine locations on popular mapping services, use digital cameras for documentation, and edit photographs on computers. The point, however, is that the use of these technologies is not significant for the artistic outcome. To draw a comparison, the fact that Nancy Holt probably drove rather than rode a horse to the Great Basin Desert to make her *Sun Tunnels* (1973–1976) does not ultimately change the nature of her work, and therefore disqualifies the automotive technology relevant to appreciating her art work.

Secondly, rare are the artists who seem to focus on digital technologies as the subject of their work. Since the 1960s, the set of issues related to the environment and addressed in environmental artworks has grown steadily. Although many artists remain unconcerned with the social dimension and prefer to concentrate on materials, Goldsworthy being the archetype, many artists have taken the environment in a broader sense than just a physical reality.

PAIKKA

The many reflections on physical, social and political borders are good examples of works in which the environment is understood in its many dimensions. And yet, there are but few examples in which artists would reflect on the direct or indirect impact of digital technologies on the environment. It would take too long to propose explanations for this relative indifference. Intuitively, one can assume that there is a tropism for certain social issues such as pollution and its remediation, and that digital technologies as a social phenomenon does not fall into the traditional realm of environmental art.

Although the sole case of digital technologies is addressed, the short development above reveals the heavy weight of legacy for environmental artists. It seems to be difficult to make use of computers or related tools in the art practice, and the deep social modifications induced by the transition into the informational age seem not to be among the prime concerns of artists. As such, this is not to be deplored. In the end, many photographers still make black-and-white analogue pictures, which is more than a century old technology, and it does not undermine the quality of their work. Why then should environmental artists, unlike photographers, pay particular attention to digital technologies? Our main argument revolves around the assumed ambition of environmental art to achieve greater inclusion between person and place.

VAI

Among the many possibilities offered by digital technologies is the un-precedented potential for interaction. Sensors and computing power offer a wide set of solutions to artists willing to empower their audience in their experience of the art. Examples of such interactions are found mostly in works customarily labelled as computer art. This does not mean, however, that all interactive art is computer art. One can also accept that some artworks fall into several categories. Once more, categorisation does not have a purpose of its own, but it is only a tool for aesthetic appreciation. Among many examples, the work *Night Lights* (2010), by collective YesYesNo and associated partners, consists of a large projection onto a building, computed after the movements of the audience on two stages, the tracking of mobile phone waves, and hand interaction above a light table. This type of work never appear in publications, websites or critical essays about environmental art, although it would comply with many of the definitions of environmental art. To remain within the boundaries of this article, "*Night Lights*" clearly enhances the sense of inclusion between person and place: while the feel of the latter continuously changes according to the movements of the former, the artwork embedded in the place has a direct effect on the behaviour of passers-by.

TILA

Another potential array of innovation for environmental art is the use of digital technologies in documentation. One will remember that among the ambitions of early land artists was that of breaking out of the gallery space, leading them to carry out large-scale works in remote locations and subsequently to pay particular attention to documentation. In some cases, such as Fulton's walks, documentation is the only possible mode of confrontation with the audience. Despite this original ambition, it must be noted that the movement became largely institutionalised and that, quite ironically, documents of early land art works became collectibles. Institutionalisation is rather a natural move and may be unavoidable for artists willing to live outside their work. Among other functions, art institutions have an economic purpose, as they are means of legitimation, organise rarity, monopolise the display of art or its documentation, hamper reproduction, and ultimately give value to selected works or artists. Despite this context, some artists may still be willing to (also) work outside the said institutions. For a long time, this was almost impossible, because of the monopoly of diffusion channels enjoyed by a few powerful actors. Today, this monopoly, in the field of visual arts as in others, is radically challenged by the Internet and other digital networks. In the case of artworks that are site-specific, the potential impact of new modes of diffusion is probably more significant for the documentation of art than for the artwork itself, although it is sometimes difficult to draw a line between the two. In any case, digital networks lead to rethinking the very concept of documentation. Because of today's ubiquity of information, artists have the potential to abolish the time sequence between the production phase and the display of documentation, both with the potential to happen concomitantly. In addition, the artists can bypass intermediaries, would these be publishers or gallery owners, and thus free themselves from their format constraints. Last but not least, the form of documentation can be rethought in order to enhance the sense of inclusion between person and place. *Double Negative* (1969–1970) is an artwork concerned with the direct physical experience of our bodies in relation to the landscape. However, the documents through which most of us know it consists of aerial photographs, appealing to our intellect more than to any of our senses, to grasp the aesthetic experience the artwork provides. In the end, the documentation of the work, because of its very form, jeopardizes the initial ambition of the artist. This can be overcome by using new forms of documentation. The use of photography is sometimes justified as offering a faithful account of reality. One can ask of which reality, or rather of which experience of reality. As with any other media, photography is not neutral and suggests particular aesthetic responses from the viewer. Digital technologies widen the set of options available to artists for the documentation of their work, and possibly offer the possibility to trigger alternative aesthetic experiences in the distant gaze suggested by most forms of documentation in environmental art. In a recent work entitled *Down River Vashka* (2013) and carried out in collaboration with a linguist, I built a bark with a local boat builder in northern Russia and went down a river for a few hundred kilometres, collecting stories from the few persons we met on the way. The documentary part (rather than documentation) of the work consists of a series of small boxes displayed in a way that is reminiscent of the large meanders typical of the rivers flowing in northern Russia. When the viewer opens a box, it triggers the playing of an interview for which no translation is available, but whose topic can be understood with the content of the box. For that purpose, I used simple micro-electronics and hacked a popular media player. Such tools make it possible to integrate sound samples in the installation and incite the audience to use their many senses, while preserving the general feeling of my work, which does not include any apparent electronic device such as earphones, MP3 player, or screen. My goal was to provide a more faithful account of my journey than photography or text would: I had but a vague idea about the topics of the stories I was told, and it demanded effort on my side to access the cultural dimension of the landscape.

A last dimension that should be taken into account when considering environmental art and digital technologies is the treatment of these technologies as a subject matter of artworks. We have mentioned that digital technologies became a significant factor shaping our environment. As such, they are as eligible as industrialism, the human-nature relationship or the political organisation of space as subject matter of environmental artworks. In fact, many artists have treated them in their artworks, but these are only seldom interpreted, criticised and displayed from an environmental art perspective. For example, Aram Bartholl's work deals with "geo services", such as Google Maps. As such, his work is directly concerned with the environment and the way we apprehend it. Besides, the physical characteristics of his art makes it completely eligible as environmental art. In *Google Portrait Series* (2007–2009), Bartholl painted QR codes representing the different Google searches of his name in various countries, pointing out the geographical relativity of our digital identities. In yet another work, *Map* (2010), he installed a giant pin in Taipei, mimicking those found on Google Maps. This last work should fit the definitions, putting the emphasis on material criteria. And yet he and other artists working in public space and addressing stringent aspects of contemporary environments are rarely considered in environmental art.

In the light of the few arguments developed in this paper, the case of digital technologies reveals a strong continuity both in terms of themes and of forms in environmental art works. Although there may be arguments against the use of digital technologies, for instance some critics suggest that they deprive the artist of control over their own work, they also have the potential to renew the original ambition of environmental art, which is to promote a more inclusive mode of aesthetic experience than the traditional distant gaze.

What is suggested, however, is that the problem may not be a rejection of digital technologies by the artists themselves. In fact, there are dozens of examples of pieces dealing with the environment while using digital technologies. However, they are rarely recognised as environmental art. In the end, artists usually make their art, whatever that would be, without consideration for categorisations and norms. The problem may rather come from the attitude of other actors, such as members of the academy, curators and the audience, whose understanding of environmental art may remain strongly conditioned by the legacy of past decades.

Despite this observation, I still hope to witness some evolution in our general attitude towards environmental art. Like many members of my generation, I learnt to use the computer keyboard before I knew how to write with a pen. This is to say that computers, like myself and my earthly container, have already been around for a while, and it may be time for environmental art to take them into consideration. Instead, digital technologies seem to have gone almost unnoticed. *Land and Environmental Art*, edited by Jeffrey Kastner, probably the most popular anthology on the subject, was first published in 1998. This was the book through which I was introduced to the movement during my studies. With a few exceptions, all the works presented in it precede the boom of digital technologies. It includes no more than one single work making open use of digital technologies: *Ocean Earth: Processed Imagery from AVHRR of the North Sea* (1988) by Peter Fend. With all the respect I have for the artist, I believe there are more poetic, more interesting and more significant works making use of digital technologies than a time-lapse satellite image of the explosion of algae bloom around the Danish peninsula. I wish we could now leave Kastner's book to collect dust on the shelf and adopt a new, more up-to-date "bible", because the world did not stop in 1990. To my knowledge, there is no such calculation, which makes me hope that some bold and daring authors will soon publish the long awaited *Land and Environmental Art – Updated*.

The Gaze

Laura
Uimonen

The Gaze

May I take you for a walk? Accompanying us will be Markku Hakuri, Master of Political Science, artist and emeritus professor, whom I got to know in the early years of the new millennium. You may borrow Hakuri's gaze, like a pair of binoculars, albeit via my memory and what I have learned.

"I like to give writers a free hand", says Markku, when asking us to write about the teaching of environmental art at the University of Art and Design Helsinki. This is so like Markku! His idea of freedom always comes with a sense of responsibility, and an unspoken expectation of surprise, ambition and pursuit of meaningfulness. Since I consider walking to be an essential mode of existing and perceiving the environment, I will picture us taking a walk. I would like to remind you of how walking actually works as a way of storing places in our corporeal memory. I will take you for a walk based on my memory. My aids are images and notebooks from 2001 to 2004. Many of the images are slides, so you may hear the hum and clicks of a slide projector as we walk.

Imagine and dream with me, because imagination has a special significance in environmental art. As a professor of environmental art, Hakuri resembles the authors that Gaston Bachelard writes about in his work *La poétique de l'espace* (*The Poetics of Space*), 1957. Bachelard's text offers keys to the ideas in Hakuri's art and teaching, as Bachelard uses works of art, poems and stories to open a view to a maze in which everyday human life is intertwined with dreams, fairy tales and meanings reinforced through art. Every detail or thing 'speaks' to us. According to Bachelard, art is a duplication of life, competing with life by setting up surprises that excite our consciousness and prevent it from falling asleep.[1] *La poétique de l'espace*, a work that artists and architects will be quite familiar with, was not translated into Finnish until 2003. The translation was introduced as part of the reading material for students of environmental art. The Finnish translator Tarja Roinila (2003: 17) sums up Bachelard's premises in the foreword: "Without an ability to be enthralled, the examination of a work of art is dead, be it descriptive, analytical or evaluative". It was precisely enthralment that Hakuri expected from environmental art students.

Our walk sort of starts at the waiting room of the main railway station, which is where many of us change to get to our offices in Arabianranta. Hakuri's gaze pierces into the everyday scenes at the waiting room, witnessing beauty, cruelty, truth, injustice, movement and rhythm. The gaze captures people's steps at

[1] Bachelard [1957] 2003: 61.

the station, the mind captures the recorded announcements, the clink of a coin and a stranger's gaze, averted and fixed on the wall of white tiles.

The mind has started walking, as the tram rattles towards Arabianranta and the University of Art and Design Helsinki, which is where our joint walk will begin. Our task is to sense places, as the premise of the introductory courses in environmental art, was, in Bachelard's terms, a kind of 'topoanalysis'. In Bachelard's topoanalysis, the task of a place is to store and condense time, and the analysis itself focuses on the psychological study of the sites of our intimate lives (translation 1964 by Maria Jolas).[2] We must therefore sense, remember, imagine, pass through and, above all, live places. The full experience, including images, smells, tastes, sounds, feelings, memories, details and associations, is captured by the artist's gaze, actions and perhaps, ultimately, also their works. The first questions on our walk could be: is asphalt beautiful? Why does the soil not breathe under the asphalt? Who is licensed to suffocate things? Who walked here before me?

From the Hämeentie road, we walk toward the waterfront, which in the early 2000s underwent a transformation from an area of contaminated land to a residential neighbourhood. The Vanhankaupunginlahti bay combines residential areas from different eras, a historical factory area and the Lammassaari island, forgotten in the middle of the bay and accessible via a duckboard walkway. We walk past a block of flats, with a human-sized nest high on its outer wall. Bachelard would call this an image of inhabiting[3] I look up and I think of security, a look down from the nest into the street and onto the glazed balconies of the new buildings, and the green tram winding through the street. Hakuri, in turn, may have been thinking about nest-building, homecoming or looking safely over the bay from the nest: it is a work by him, entitled *Tuulenpesä* (*Witchbroom*), from 2007, located on Birger Kaipiaisen katu, and it hides the 'cooling-off terrace' of a communal sauna.[4]

We continue along the shoreline, through the Vanhakaupunki area towards Viikki. We put on helmets and descend, floor by floor, underground and into the rocky depths, into the basement! Hakuri wants to treat us to an encounter with the basics. A water purification plant built deep into the rock conveys the waste-water of Helsinki residents in open channels. Near the bar screen, we can see a collection of objects that have ended up in the sewer: toys, false teeth and combs.

When underground, we cannot escape the spectacle of darkness and descent, which is significant in itself, a transition into something out of the ordinary, from the light into the dark and from the open to the closed. The idea is to awaken us to responsibility and draw it onto our bodies as a concrete experience. The flowing, bubbling sewage does not appear dreamy, but silently asks: "Did you know?" The human smell clings to our clothes, and we are forced to breathe in

[2] Bachelard [1957] 2003: 82–84.

[3] Bachelard [1957] 2003: 220.

[4] Tuula Isohanni [2007: 28] *Art in Arabian-ranta. Art collaboration 2000-2011.* World Design Capital Helsinki 2012.

Basic Course 2008, Helsinki, Finland

the smell while walking the long corridors. In Bachelard's terms, we are in the cellar of a house of dreams, which is connected to a whole host of ideas of child-hood fears, bundles of corridors and roots of cities underground. Drama and exaggerated fear live underground. [5]

Because our basement can be extended through our imagination, we walk underground until we reach the Hakaniemi area, where we emerge from the metro tunnel to encounter another urban staple, the town square. An example of the ancient centres of towns forces us to think about the public space and our need to meet people. The students attending the introductory course in environmental art are supplied with brown paper, buckets, and rolls of thick clear plastic. Working with Hakuri is a serious game, in which the rules must be justified. There is humour and a trace of a smile in the game, but there is also the reverse side: tears, sadness, war, loss, concern and violence. The assignments explore dreams, secrets and promises.

The white buckets and the square. The buckets will become an urban garden patch for carrots. One group is challenging the others, as a human chain is transferring water from one bucket to the other, from one end of Hakaniemi to the other, from bay to bay. From the edge of the square, we ascend into high-rise buildings. The corridors are narrow and dark. In the hands of the students, the brown paper turns into love letters to the residents of the buildings, and the students distribute them directly into the letter boxes. Another group twists the paper into a rope ladder, which can be used to escape to the sea. The ladder swaying on the waves is attached to a railing in the seawall. The plastic is used to comment on the sculpture *Maailman rauha* (World Peace). Students use ropes to pull a plastic globe in different directions. As the evening falls, plastic is being twisted into nests for light on the shore of Kaisaniemi. In the middle of our course day, the security guards on duty in Hakaniemi square begin to question us making art. Hakuri negotiates with them, and we can continue our walk. The more regular troublemakers in the square continue with their daily routines.

Close your eyes. We take a step and suddenly we are in the municipality of Tuusula. Our fellow walkers are a group of students from the University of Art and Design Helsinki and the Department of Architecture at the Helsinki University of Technology. This time, the theme of our walk is the third environmental fundament, La Strada. In Tuusula, we can witness the coexistence of the new and the old, the hand-built houses nicely sited in the landscape and the new industrial urban developments, which is typical of Finnish built environments.

[5] Bachelard [1957] 2003: 99-103.

We first take the lakeside road that meanders between forest patches, villas and fields. Students ask, confused, how to touch the environment that is inter-woven with the life stories, artists' homes and works of Halonen, Soldan-Brofelt,

Aho and Sibelius? The walk combines the old with the new, as we stroll along the side of the Järvenpääntie road. The road is familiar in its ordinariness; it cuts through the landscape, loud and straight; there are cars swooshing by. In its subways, the concrete radiates coldness, and there is a rank smell.

The works of art proposed by the students included creating silhouettes of the birds prevalent along the lakeside road on the tops of the old electricity poles, and painting the subways of the new road in bright colours. A third memorable proposal was possibly the most important in the eyes of Hakuri. The maker of the proposal suggested that an ordinary blue-and-white road sign be set up at the side of the Järvenpääntie road, with the text "poems hidden under road surface". The proposal refers to Henri David Thoreau's essay *Walking*. We, too, could insist with Thoreau: "We should go forth on the shortest walk, perchance, in the spirit of undying adventure, never to return, prepared to send back our embalmed hearts only as relics to our desolate kingdoms."[6] Art has the power to add the imagined, the dreamt to the landscape.

On the La Strada course, we explored the roadside environment by walking, photographing and drawing. I knew this practice from architecture, but on this walk, we are allowed to meander, to stop and reflect without a plan, and, while walking, we are allowed to close our eyes, listen and breathe in the smells. The gaze can be blown wide open, and we can look directly, without expecting to arrive at a predetermined result.

We can spot an important perspective related to places from the early years of environmental art education: movement. The first course, realised in Tuusula, and the related seminar spurred a debate in our work community on people's daily movements and the connection between places and ways of movement. There is no need to prove whether the courses led to movement-related research projects or whether researchers introduced themes that interest them into art education, but they are both linked to the connection between societal structures and everyday life. After Thoreau's ideas on walking, students were introduced to touring artists, nature photographers and people who occupy urban or agrarian space. Other themes of the environmental art courses included noise, migration and experiences of the changing environment.

Close your eyes again. We are in the village of Kellokoski, near the old power plant. We are walking around the light multifaceted industrial building, passing locked doors. If you read to yourself all the texts that we pass on our way, you will hear one work of art that was created here. In the work, you can hear words from the writings on the wall, and the chant 'abloy, abloy, abloy'. Take one more step, and it's a winter's night in Kellokoski. The building is covered in multi-coloured light and seems to be changing its shape. Warm light glows from behind blocks of ice. We are joined by a group of students

[6] Thoreau 1862/1998: 7. Translated into Finnish by Markku Envall.

43

PAIKKA

from around the world. The snow under our feet is new and crunchy. The ice is exotic, cold and dangerously slippery. Take yet another step, and it is summer, but there are ice cubes in the courtyard, with a photograph printed on their surface.

What can art add to a place, or can art succeed in becoming a part of a place? Bachelard's ideas include a proposal on how we, when stopping, when standing still, could be elsewhere and could dream in an immeasurable world. Bachelard explains his idea by giving, as an example, a forest in which we may feel that we are sinking into a boundless world.[7] Could a work of art stop us and make us dream?

[7] Bachelard 382–383. Translated into Finnish by Tarja Roinila.

The final step back to where we started: the Töölönlahti bay, the Linnun-laulu area and the trackside. Soon, the lights will be lit and the sky will be dark. Once again, we meet the students, whose task this time is to build themselves a temporary shelter and spend a night in it. Hakuri reminds us that in most cases, environmental art is an act rather than an object. Many students choose to hide, and their works are camouflaged in the urban space. No-one may notice that there is an arts student spending the night in a waste paper bin or a shelter made to look like a street cabinet. The most memorable act is a female student sheltering in a burka. The body and the face are hidden from the gaze, but the student must keep moving through the night, staying alert and aware of the threats. Her act reminds us of the safety of our environment, our freedom and the level of privacy allowed, all of which art, perhaps, only encounters outside the galleries. We return to the station, the walk is over. Smoke puffs from under the curtain, chug-chug, chug-chug. The sky is lit up with stars.

—

11 July 2013: At home on Laiduntie, when the dog is waking up and the poppy plant has opened its red-orange petals to sway in the wind.

REFERENCES

Bachelard, Gaston [1957] 2003. *Tilan poetiikka.* Nemo: Helsinki. Finnish translation and foreword by Tarja Roinila. Original title La poétique de l´espace [The Poetics of Space]. Presses Universitaires de France.
Isohanni, Tuula 2012. *Art in Arabianranta. Art collaboration 2001–2011.* Helsingin talous- ja suunnittelukeskuksen julkaisuja [Publications of the city of Helsinki economic and planning centre] 4/2011: Helsinki.
Thoreau, Henry David [1862] 1998. *Kävelemisen taito.* Jack-in-the-box: Helsinki. Finnish translation by Markku Envall. Original title *Walking* in the June issue of The Atlantic Monthly.

Yhteistyö
yliopistojen kanssa

Collaboration
with Universities

TAIVAS

AED1906

RNV1930

Taivas / Heaven 2009, Tallinn, Estonia

Put Yourself in the Right Place 2013, Lund University, Sweden

Pelit / Games 2003, Middlebury College, Vermont, USA

Mingdaon lapiot / Mingdao's shovels 2009, Tsinghua University, Beijing, China

Rakenteilla / Under Construction 2009, Tsinghua University, Beijing, China

Läpimärkä / The Flood Wet to Skin 2009,
University of Helsinki, Finland

Jokapäiväinen leipäsi / Your Daily Bread 2009,
University of Helsinki, Finland

Picnic 2012, University of Helsinki, Finland

Tarkkailija / Observer 2003, Middlebury Gollege, Vermont, USA

Seinämä / The Wall 2003, Middlebury College, Vermont, USA

Threshold: Locating the Environment

Scott Andrew
Elliott

Threshold:
Locating the Environment

Threshold: A border or point that must be crossed to move from one space to another, a space in-between; a degree of intensity, a limit below which a phenomenon is not perceptible or above which a sensation can no longer be sustained.

Over the course of the past eight years, I have been involved in the Environmental Art Programme as a student and as a teacher. During this time, I have attempted to determine how environmental artworks function, in what realm and for what reason. One question often arises: where are environmental artworks placed? Where is this 'environment'? It is clear that although the Land Art movement of the late 1960s established a definitive direction away from galleries and museums, for the field of environmental art this was neither the beginning nor the end. Environmental artworks exist in natural landscapes of all sorts, as well as in urban landscapes and inside architectural structures of all kinds, including galleries and museums. The then question remains, where is this environment?

Environmental artworks exist in a liminal area, an in-between zone, and manipulate the threshold of what is experienced as the separation between the world and the work of art. The experience of environmental artworks commingles with one's experience of what is tentatively referred to as real world, the world of everyday life, and creates links with contexts that lend to their meaning. This situating of environmental artworks in this liminal area is, in part, in order to subvert the manipulative control of the art venue in all its productive qualities and preconditioning of an art experience. As a result of being placed within this in-between zone, and by manipulating this threshold, works of environmental art are able to produce experiences that challenge social norms, behaviours or opinion, and evoke a critical rethinking of such topics within a context that is most present and, as a result, relevant to one's experience and understanding of the quotidian. This also demands a rethinking of philosophical, ethical, and moral questions.

In order to better grasp the current and future forms of environmental art practice, it is important to establish where it came from. Determining the point at which environmental art became a form in the history art, or when it became part of the critical discourse that includes the art world, is a contentious endeavour. This starting point is a slippery one to grasp, as environmental art

has become a kind of umbrella term or catch-all that could be applied to
a vast and variable conglomerate of creative practices. One remaining trace
of the original inspirations towards its formation is the intention to create, show,
and perform works outside the gallery or museum, and to seek value as part of
a public discourse separate from the power of these institutions which isolate
artworks from contextualising relations. These institutions attribute value to
artworks as art objects, functioning in that way as art-making-machines, which
are able to transform any object displayed within them into a work of art
through this attribution of value.

This movement away from galleries and museums was perhaps in response
to the development of the white cube as a space for displaying art [O'Doherty]. That
is, its manner of separating an artwork from any context, any history, situating
it in a timeless space in order to eliminate any chance for an external influence
on one's experience of that work. Social contexts, political contexts, situational
contexts, all such contexts that could contribute to one's interpretation of
a work of art were removed in order to create a sacred space for viewing works
of art. Environmental art returns to this plethora of contexts and relations that
establish a situation and material that call to attention a viewer's experience of
the world. By actively engaging with these contexts, environmental artists have
created artworks that are in no way kept separate from quotidian reality, and as
a result evoke an experience of art that is phenomenologically distinct from
what one might experience in a gallery or museum setting.

In '*Cultural Hijack: Rethinking Intervention*', Ben Parry outlines what is
the difference between experiencing a work of environmental art, in the world
of everyday real-life experience, and experiencing a work of gallery art:

> 'In this instance, a non-determined participant is
> treated to a real-life experience of the artist's intervention
> that blurs distinctions, defies categorization and is free of
> art history and criticism. When such a work is repositioned
> in the gallery, this experience is missing and a more precise
> understanding is transformed into a *relic* or tangible object;
> photographs, maps, sound, drawings. In the gallery context
> the public is treated to a reframing of the event that inevitably
> asserts its identity as 'art', relating it back to the chronology
> of art history.' [Parry, p. 19]

In my opinion, works of environmental art are not separate from art history
and criticism, as there is a clear history of artists who have made artworks in
this realm and one who encounters such a work today may be aware of this art

historical context. The difference arises through the fact that, as the artwork is closer to one's everyday experience of the world, it relates to different contexts than it would if in an art gallery. In the gallery, the only context is art history. In the world at large, it can connect to this plethora of contexts, affording meanings and interpretations impossible within a gallery, and need not reference this art historical context if so desired. This situation offers the possibility of connection to varied contexts, and as such affords a variety of readings and interpretations, which is something not afforded by a situation within an art gallery[1].

In 2004, Peter McCaughey created a project for the Liverpool Biennial in collaboration with Jump Ship Rat. This project took an abandoned and disaffected cinema in the centre of Liverpool and re-opened it by installing CCTV video cameras around the cinema. These cameras relayed images of the interior of the space, including performances on stage by local musicians and poets, onto a glass screen that blocked the entrance to the cinema. This urban intervention, according to McCaughey, "was delivered in public, unannounced, unnamed", and it was this situation that effected meaning in the project. Passers-by could encounter this project while on their way to work, and include the experience as somehow part of their daily activities and routines. It would interrupt their experience of the world, if they noticed it, by interjecting visions of a forgotten space, perhaps evoking memories of going to that long-closed cinema in their youth, or at the least offer a moment of pause and inspire curiosity. Without requesting permission or even informing the artist, the Liverpool Biennial organisers placed two large orange cubes with their marketing logo on the exterior of this cinema after McCaughey had completed his work. McCaughey writes, "I see that as tantamount to sticking a post-it on a painting, declaring 'Art Here'" McCaughey, p. 73. I was lucky enough to be present that day, and proudly assisted McCaughey as he took a sledgehammer to those orange cubes, destroying this curatorial "post-it". This violent act removed his work from the realm in which it was demarcated as "art", and returned it to its intended realm, this in-between space that is closer to, if not part of, an everyday experience of the world. The violence was very much needed, and as a statement, this action has had a strong effect on my understanding of environmental art and where its environment is. This was a key moment in my own artistic development, and was an experience that inspired me to apply to

[1] Though some environmental artworks have been sited within art galleries, they focus on this situational context, on this productive nature of the gallery, and comment on this mechanism by making apparent its manner of attributing value. Environmental artworks in galleries do often create immersive worlds of their own, separating one from the gallery and, as a result, establishing another world of contexts and relations.

PAIKKA

the Environmental Art Programme, and I kept a piece of one orange cube as a relic that serves to remind me of my priorities and ethics in creating works of art.

If the environment of environmental art is this threshold, what, then, is the effect of placing artworks here? In his lecture at the Reversible Destiny Conference (2008), Jondi Keane discusses threshold in reference to the work of Arakawa and Gins, and in particular their project *Ubiquitous Site: Nagi's Ryoanji*, located in Nagi, Japan. This work consists of a concrete cylinder that is tipped on its horizontal plane, and within which mirrored Zen gardens run the length of the cylinder. A sense of true gravitational vertical is difficult to grasp as a result of this tipping, and the mirroring and placement of these gardens further confuse one's sense of what is up and what is down, complicating understanding of one's orientation in the world.

Keane discusses the use of the Zen gardens in *Ubiquitous Site*, as a response to the Zen Buddhist gardens at Ryoan-ji, Japan, to illustrate a situation similar to the experience of artworks within a gallery or museum white cube. Ryoanji, an 11th Century Zen Buddhist temple near Kyoto, Japan, contains a Zen garden that is designed in such a way that one is only able to see the garden from a viewing platform that is raised and set back from the garden. One is not permitted to enter the garden, to walk around the rocks, to experience the materiality of the raked sand. He describes how the viewing platform is set back and above this garden, so that one is able to sit and contemplate it only from a distance, but is never granted access to a direct experience of this garden, of the materiality of the rocks, the lines raked in the sand, the manicured shrubs. In contrast to this, the Zen gardens included in *Ubiquitous Site* place one within the gardens. The difference effected by this immersion within the space is that it:

> 'puts you in the centre of this world-creation, establishes you in
> the middle of the creation of the world; there is no separation,
> there is no observation. The world is not something out there
> that is to be accessed and brought in to you, or that you reach
> out to and participate with, but rather you are constantly in
> the process of building the world, of creating the world, and
> through this on going process of world-making we bring the
> world into being along with bringing ourselves into being.' [Keane]

This moves one from the position of observer, beyond the position of participant, and into a position as co-creator of the world. Moving from being separated by a threshold, by a spatial division separating viewer and object, one enters this threshold and sustains an experience within it. This threshold becomes the location for both the work and oneself, the location

VAI

TILA

Shelter workshop 2001, Helsinki, Finland

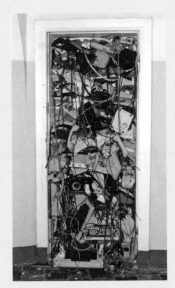

Breaking into Prison workshop 2009, Tallinn, Estonia

PAIKKA

for a "process of world-making", a co-creation at the same time as a co-emergence of being, and it is this experience that is the work of environmental art.

Situating a work of art in this threshold has the effect of changing one's position in relation to the artwork. No longer creating a subject-object relationship, this placement makes apparent the process of world-making that we are constantly taking up. This process occurs not only when co-creating a work of environmental art, but it occurs constantly, at all times, in all aspects of living-being-in-the-world. It is either unconscious, below a threshold of perception or awareness, or otherwise hidden from us. Through an experience of environmental art that makes apparent this process of co-creation, co-emergence, world-making, one can become consciously aware of this process, which is essential to our way of being-in-the-world, our way of living in environments.

Parry writes about the way that the "public" is involved in this co-creation of environmental artworks:

VAI

> 'Transforming the 'public' into a series of individual
> collaborators creates a multiplicity of meanings
> and a complexity of social relations that in turn disrupt
> conventions of public space and stable notions of the public.
> This notion of the public as collaborator or active co-producer
> of the artwork or intervention is vital in thinking about
> a radical art that blurs the distinction between artist and
> public, between art and everyday life.' Parry, p. 28-29

It is this blurring of the distinction between artist and public, and between art and everyday life, that situates environmental art in this threshold. It is the placement within this threshold that calls to attention our human action of world-making, as creative beings, be it in the creation of works of art or in the act of experiencing the world.

The Environmental Art Programme has been researching the relation of an artwork to its environment through workshops that require students to create environmental artworks in locations that are filled with contexts and histories. "Shelter" (Marco Casagrande and Sami Rintala 2001) gave students the task to spend a night outdoors in Helsinki, in a shelter they each made. These students had to take into consideration their own needs for this task, as well as what part of the city would afford them a place. Furthermore, the workshop required them to place themselves in the city, to understand its local contexts, geography, materials, and as a result their relation to the city.

TILA

"Breaking into Prison" (Scott Andrew Elliott 2009) presented students with an abandoned prison in Estonia, originally built as a Russian military fort and transformed into a prison during the Soviet era. Students were required to make interventions into the site by investigating its history, and were permitted to only re-organise materials found within the prison, not to bring in materials from outside. This process developed a way of analysing a site, and used artistic practice as a way to investigate the history and meaning of a place, as well as one's relation to it. Furthermore, the experience of the artworks was such that it was difficult to determine which prison cells were made into artworks, and which were not.

The pedagogical philosophy of the Environmental Art Programme has deepened the understanding of what an environment is, through the artworks produced and the creative practices invented by students. Through siting artworks in this liminal zone, this threshold, a questioning of contexts engenders new resolutions, seeks out new answers, and produces more precise questions. As a product of this programme, new sites for artworks and for creative practices have been established through this process of constantly redefining what is "environment", and what the environment for works of art could be.

The environment for environmental art may be the threshold outlined in this chapter, but it most certainly will not exist as the sole environment. Further development of this field should outline multiple thresholds as environments, or techniques of thresholding, to establish even more possibilities for new forms of art and new ways of being.

REFERENCES

Keane, Jondi. "The Land[ing] of Endeavour." *Reversible Destiny: Declaration of the Right Not to Die, the Second International Arakawa and Gins, Architecture and Philosophy Conference/Congress* held at the University of Pennsylvania and the Slought Foundation from April 4-6 2008.

McCaughey, Peter. "Not Untitled." *Cultural Hijack: Rethinking Intervention.* Ed. Ben Parry. Liverpool: Liverpool University Press and Jump Ship Rat, 2011, p. 48-78. Print.

O'Doherty, Brian. *Inside the White Cube: The Ideology of the Gallery.* Berkeley: University of California Press, 1976. Print.

Parry, Ben. "Rethinking Intervention." *Cultural Hijack: Rethinking Intervention.* Ed. Ben Parry. Liverpool: Liverpool University Press and Jump Ship Rat, 2011, p. 10-38. Print.

Functionality of Meaning in Environmental Art

Expanding on some footnotes[1]

Jan Kenneth Weckman

Functionality of Meaning
in Environmental Art

— Expanding on some footnotes[1]

*The culture industry turns into public relations, the manufacturing of `goodwill'
per se, without regard for particular firms or saleable objects. Brought to bear is
a general uncritical consensus, advertisements produced for the world, so that each
product of the culture industry becomes its own advertisement.*[2]

    - Theodor Adorno

In 2007, a tsunami of fusing of educations in art, design, architecture,
technology and economy together made my former teaching campus vanish
from the Finnish educational scenery, and more specifically, from the scene
of visual culture in Helsinki. Consider this, however, only as a virtual vanishing
feat, similar to linguistic change. The dots are there on paper still, but in another
order. What follows, when language is destroyed, is, from another point of view,
only another language. But, one might ask, what will the language say? Have we
ever encountered a being that is language? Yes, we have. It is called marketing,
a form, perhaps *the* form, of the culture industry.[3]

    Still, something interesting is *taking its place.* Aalto University in Helsinki
announced recently, against all odds, that criteria for both artistic research and
perhaps art, as well as for its quality and value, should be established once more
in efforts to develop *a more argumentative mode of research like that of science
instead of ad-hoc impressions and myths.*[4] This piece of news does not fall from
the heavens. The post-Bologna situation in European higher education, with
BA+MA+PhD level studies at colleges, now universities, created out of former
polytechnic institutions (teaching art, design and media), makes for a veritable
battleground between discourses searching for decisive criteria that can be
shown to sponsors. Until its *demenagement* into Aalto University in 2008, the
former University of Art and Design Helsinki, (UIAH) entered a pressure can
of academicalization, if not medicalization, during the 1990s, with art history,
science, aesthetics, design theory and new media as *pharmakon.*[5] Modernist
fine art, having held its place as a model of visual thinking until then, did not
easily fit into such a cause, regardless of the fact that elevating an applied arts

school to a university during the next decade, simultaneously, saw the birth of new Higher Education programs for artists *in spe* (Pallas MA in 1995, and Environmental Art MA, in 2000). These developments seem to have been fueled by a miscalculated idea about the place of visual arts surrendering to the cultural industry, as it were.[6] But, exactly this predicament, I will propose, illustrates public art, as well.[7]

In order to expand the view of the various ways to approach environmental art as part of the public domain, a contextual trip in the bag of the reception and methods of inquiry concerning environmental art should be in order. To illustrate the conflict of contemporary art moving into a new position, into that of "functional" public design, some environmental art degree work I had an opportunity to review, as an outside reviewer, will highlight the confusing situation. Painting such a picture needs its backdrop, a deeper landscape that will consist of a few references to near-classic theorists on environment and public art, Miwon Kwon and James Meyer. The latter writer will give me, in the first place, a reason to renew the acquaintance with "functionality" that was supposed to be forgotten when discussing art *überhaupt*.[8]

Adorno did not have in mind the various ways in which art might disappear. But he conceived a general model of the enemy, art as culture industry.[9] This pertains to, say, power structures in public art; the site of the *Öffentlichkeit*, as such, surely defines conditions for all cultural strivings that find their being at least in my view in an ontology of communication and rhetoric. In fact, I am not able to solve the question on the culture industry looming over our heads in contemporary art in general, but will assume that the shadow grows visibly stronger in public art. Adorno is then a silent umbrella over my thoughts.

Scandinavian modernism can well be defined as a hidden struggle to sustain autonomous fields of visual professions, those of architects, engineers, designers and artists (not photographers, for heaven's sake, in those days). Of these, artists surely tend to be included as a minor actor, while lip service is paid to creativity and art in general, regardless of who is speaking. Nothing really fundamental can be said against such a smoke curtain. Art is like a perfume all over the place.

But, if we agree that the work of art is eventually something virtual without being outside the social, all communication overlap in habits and tendencies that we share artists and non-artists alike.[10] Miwon Kwon offers a set-up from which to start.[11] Kwon's theoretical edge brings up a shifting perspective on public art. Kwon presents a current ongoing development, given the feasibility of generalizing from American art, during the last forty years, which moves from 1) art in public places, to include 2) art as public spaces, onwards to 3) art in the public interest. This is obviously not a linear but a widening range of practices, while the cutting-edge description advances, as always, more in a linear form, so as to race towards the new. The European scenery surely must differ, left to further study, however, in order to pick the historical initiative of the earth-art as a backdrop for the contemporary situation. Making a hypothetical guess, that "Continental" interests are strongly inclined toward art-as-research and identity politics, a more detailed survey of Kwon's third development should ask the question about whose interest public interest works for? Kwon rightly points to the difference between "progressive" art and "progressive" politics.

Above, I mentioned the seemingly contradictory evolution by the University of Art and Design Helsinki, against the tide of both academicalization and design professionalism getting the upper hand given the historically stronger segments of HE educations. This brings up, namely, the question, hence, of how it is possible to sustain a contemporary art as well as an environmental art MA program, programmed on the model of a history of avant-garde, on a trajectory of continuing deconstruction? The first answer is that such a set of goals within contemporary art, as has been shown, does not cringe against theorizing; on the contrary, read theoretical or critical interests that loom and flourish within the art departments of the university. Secondly, as for the Environmental Art MA program, it, in fact, followed another esteemed intention, internationalism, with regard to recruitment and openness of students and staff.

Degree work by Roel Meijs, Björn Lindström, Kaisa Salmi and Tristan Hamel, at Aalto University, are good examples of impossible outcomes considering the functionalities at play in public art. All four artists made significant comments on how to avoid product design logic invading their work. Still, all the same, one might see the environmental art work as the last outpost, past which transgress only those who go towards relational aesthetics, dialog art, or community art, exchanging their materials from the physical to the social codes and manipulating rather people in their compositions than things. In positioning environmental art – and my attention – at the seam of that something else, that will be seen as art only because of the sites where it is discussed, fulfills not only James Meyer's definition of "functional site" in his article of 1995, but goes further. If, by any chance, my attention takes on a tone of sadness in beholding the exit of art as we know it, my view is, again, only a virtual feat.

Björn Lindström
The People

Björn Lindström presents his work as *a study into the creation of a social and cultural human environment, through the Process of a Childhood Game: The Game of Building Countries' and played by the Site-Specific Childhood Playground, with adaptation in the game of a historical perspective to times ... when the natural conditions of the environment would dictate sufficiency, when human and animal muscle were the general means of power.*

Lindström, a musician and lover of Helsinki's ethnically cross-over and international music-cum-*karaoke* scene, made a move to environmental art in his attempt to redescribe his childhood feelings as well as to re-model the landscape of the seaside in the Helsinki outskirts where he lived as a child. An initial intention, the restructuring of a piece of family-owned land on the waterfront, suffered a break-down. The confrontation transformed plans for a second MA attempt, described above.

Björn Lindström creates a fictional story of a civilizations battling and negotiating with each other, builds sites and beautiful ships from natural materials, and writes an extensive script around visual objects and sites. This smacks of role-playing, romance and fiction at its core. The childhood boiler-room of almost unbearable feelings (of fear and heroism) and memories of endurance in changing seasons and climates are all hard facts of the project. When, as an adult, Lindström is getting into trouble with members of the family, he builds it into the story and undergoes redemption, *katharsis* and consolation.

This is Aristotelian theory in practice, or directly out of the handbook of Greek tragedy. We suffer with Lindström, as he does, writing the fiction about an innocent person meeting his fate, his destruction, despair or redemption. The story of Faust advances near to us as we live in the affluent society of illusions made real on an industrial scale. Lindström's fantasy project plays with the option of getting out from the here and now, while canceling the departure all the same in exchange for a piece of artwork.

Lindström's thesis work is remarkable, not only for its transparency. It contains a description of the process, together with unsuccessful attempts and misgivings. And, for sure, it contains the references to the real world. As a thesis work, something else is needed, in my opinion, other than the straightforward art project itself – which quite often stays immobile with no development. If combined with, as it should be, a report of the evolving process, to convince the reviewing panel of the capacity for contextual awareness and discursive skills of representing, analyzing and documenting the artwork, a mediocre level of success in finishing the exam contains only this.

The Feathered Sails, Espoo, Finland

Imperial Galleys investigate a burnt out Pirate ship, Espoo, Finland

A high-end result injects the artwork with a process and developing character as well. Artists should change if they study new things. Lindström tells this story.

Roel Meijs
In Situ — In Vivo

Overwhelming as the elements of nature seem to be, spatial difference has been a major field of operations for art, as well as for practically everything else. The expansion of scale continues in postmodern and contemporary art.[12] Roel Meijs recapitulates some methods of presentation and decision-making, such as chance. The work is logically two-folded in order to exist at all. A model of the site of art, being an urban interior, is needed, unless other kinds of urban sites are chosen, like those of a more distributed format, as, for example, an art magazine, a webpage, or a blog.

On the other, Meijs chooses to refrain from the white-cube aesthetics proper and uses an emptied minimarket shop where the documents and explications tell us of what goes on otherwise, in the other set-up of the work. Shown in this way, two aspects of each polarity, in *situ-in vivo*, are conjured into our experience.

Roel Meijs stresses attention toward the conceptual and social nature of the artwork. This attention has been a classic scheme within conceptual art, involving the public, starting already with the Dadaists – earlier than the arrival of the notion of environmental art. Meijs discusses his possibilities from within environmental art. Environmental art as deployment and installation of temporary objects and events is a main aspect of his theme. Meijs seems to make a work thinking about what a work of art is or could be. This is the first resulting element of his project, a reflection on the possibilities of art.

The second resulting element of the thesis project is situated well within the perimeter of what environmental art often discusses: *place identity*. Meijs takes this notion from a critical viewpoint, discussing it theoretically and socially, and, regarding the latter, saying: *Particularity of places is continually being homogenized, and commodified*, referring to Kwon (2002, 157). Meijs advances with the polarity of particularity of place (and its identity) versus homogenization. He seems to be pessimistic, referring to the Dutch poet Lucebert (1974): *Everything of value is defenceless.*

A critical voice is raised by Meijs already in the introduction, making a difference between places of utilitarian use and places where *people can use*

→ p.86

Yhteistyö — suunnittelijat ja julkinen sektori

Collaboration — Designers and Public Sector

Lentävät miehet / Flying Men 2000, Espoo, Finland

Lentävät miehet / Flying Men 2000, Espoo, Finland

Lumilyhty / Snow Lantern 2002, Tuusula, Finland

Valo virrassa / Light Stream 2002, Tuusula, Finland

Moskiittoverkko / Mosquito Curtain 2005, Helsinki, Finland

Viimeinen yhteys / Last Connection 2013, Koli, Finland

Janoinen poro / Thirsty Reindeer 2010, Seinäjoki, Finland

84

PAIKKA

a source to define themselves and to create colourful lives. The admission of personal
values and particularity being somehow defenseless is made metaphoric in the
materials and means of the project, using time-based, temporary, and non-
monumental dissolving media (papers, images, prints, balloons).

Within this second argument, elaborated above, Meijs construes two
other oppositions, where the theme of an *abstract place* and/or zero-point is
opposed to the *particularity and identity* created by finding arbitrary but specific
responses of passers-by, telling their stories about places they remember, and
communicating these to Meijs using some lines and a photograph.

The final part of the project is prepared by earlier phases and a puzzling
abstraction: a map-oriented link to the official zero-point of Helsinki, and
from there to points given by passers-by on the map of Helsinki. This takes
Meijs to a number of places where other passers-by can recapitulate each
place and its special meaning. The latter interaction is more demanding, since
participation in the work needs a photograph sent by e-mail. The answers, texts
and photographs are reproduced in the report. The nine photographs (from
20 locations in Helsinki) were eventually applied to helium balloons sent to
probable but not necessary oblivion from the official zero-point in Helsinki,
marked for graphic clarity with a red dot.

VAI

Within a range of presenting (a Deweyan notion of) art as a certain
memorable experience, the physical elements of the artwork vanish up in the
air.[13] Documents of the event/process are left in the minimarket space-gallery
for an extended display. Are these to be considered pieces of art, regenerating
the artwork in their own right, sustained by functional use of the document?
The question pinpoints a chain of mediations, all of which reach the status
of art, if they comply with historical (still in use) functions. This is the site
of display. It does "not go away", and makes an example, in itself, of a site
of remembrance and reflection.

The work of Meijs is an example of interrogating the functionalities of
public art, which are supposed to not only deconstruct our experience for what
it is worth as a modern mode of existence, but perhaps make the real work of art
vanish along the trajectory of Adorno's gaze. We should, however, also be aware
of the paradox. This is the way to go, unless we destroy art in the other direction
by fusing it with the culture industry. The Finnish proverb: *There's swamp, here's
squishy* is well formulated. My question focuses forwards, on the functionality
of deconstruction itself. Jacques Derrida, who coined deconstruction for
the academic afterworld, became an idol within architectural theory, some-
what dizzyingly for my taste. Here, the trajectory of modernism disguised as
deconstruction runs its final cause in the larger scale of architecture (which
may be used as a metaphor for public art, as well).

TILA

Architecture (theory) modeling environment (theory)

Why to use architectural discourse as a model for public art? In my opinion,
it is an obligation due to the hard facts of life; in this case, due to scale and size
that bring their bearings on our bodily life. It is only a convention to distinguish
between architecture and environment. The only difference is our virtual
knowledge of their respective difference as to the manner of having been created.

It is easy to appreciate the idealizing of architecture on professional grounds,
as when applying formal interests to solving architectural and, at least partly,
visual problems, resemblance, contrast, repetition and difference. Any painter
knows that you make three decisions simultaneously when fixing a color in
the virtual idea of a color space. The movements in this space, as in any other
space, either conform to or distinguishes themselves from something nearby,
by repetition and by difference. Fields and means of operation are not only
color directed at visual perception, but distance, scale, texture and direction/
localization. Artists and engineers know that behind textures, there are materials
and tools needed for making form fit the purpose. Materials endure all these
operations made possible only by force. The ways of responding to force differ
again and, hence, are grouped together, say, as the elements of antiquity; fire,
air, earth and water appear to us in the crude slideshow made by nature.

The expansion in size explains the delay between cubism or Malevich and
La Villette in Paris.[14] Derridean deconstruction of philosophical texts as to their
Cartesianism, or idealism-cum-reliance on logocentrism, against a general idea
of writing or against de-substantialized structure, be it signs or objects, could
be exploited readily over the chasm of constructivism/deconstruction. I bring
Peter Eisenman and Bernard Tschumi on board to place the otherness of
environmental art against a starker backlight, in order to equate the questions
on functionality with the same questions that could be addressed to architecture
and design. Seen from the sculpture studio, notably the modernist one, urban
development has utilized the heritage of Bauhaus in less than revolutionary
ways. But how little or how much, in terms of a revolutionary mood, depends
on who is among the public. Seen from the vantage point of architecture, the
autonomy of art was never there. But meaning as difference is. The classical
avant-garde agrees, there should be no rift between art and everything else.
Let us show this in new ways, not old. Why should placing deconstruction(ism)
with re-construction(ism) on the same trajectory be seen as strange?

Peter Eisenman, who was a friend of Derrida and his partner in discourse,
took the notion of deconstruction into the real world. That Eisenman could be
labeled as the Trojan horse of modernist formalism - if deconstruction was torn
out, as it were, as innocently as Helen from the ivory tower of philosophical

87

Troy, which I doubt - can be surmised rather openly from the following lines of his: *Architecture is representation of itself as construction responding to a purpose.*[15] Another line points in the same direction, *(...) forms are no longer a 'means toward an end,' (...) but an end in themselves.*[16] The first citation contains a double vision that could be stretched to apply to art as well, if we only decided on the "purpose", read function, first.[17]

In visual deconstructivism, the *corpus* shows nothing other than structure. The shift from construct to deconstruct is unseen, in contrast to its philosophical origin, which cannot be pronounced. Here, it seems, we must begin to separate structure from order or patterns of loci, like in molecular space, where left and right matters. My cryptics here refer to the corpus of Eisenman, his architectural plans. In analogy, or in reference, I use a another design student essay text by Dave Ten Hoope, Peter Eisenman - *Between method and madness*, which offers sources of Eisenman's *oeuvre*.[18] As Ten Hoope mentions, Eisenman, following the above-mentioned self-reflective formalism, refers to *House projects I–IV (page 9) while House project no X stirs the following: a number of contradictions gradually emerge in the later work (...) which finally result in the 'explosion' of the system itself. (...) the communicational notion of vertical layering, a one-way linear concept (...) with the more traditional notion of centrality: it develops aspects of both a sequential progression of space but it at the same time an investigation of centrality.* Dave Ten Hoope defines the rupture, rightly, unseen in the corpus of Eisenman. Perhaps deconstruction is itself a result of conforming to the copy-paste development of media, or about an intensification of rhythm, an acceleration of architectural planning means and speed?

Pitting student essay against student thesis, fruitful points of contact arise in my vision. For one, deconstruction is certainly always something directed towards dissecting a *corpus*, some sort of a whole. In this case, the Peter Eisenman / Bernard Tschumi pair functions, *as mutatis mutandis*, to show rather the continuation of the modernist logic within deconstruction, gone rampant and visible in a naive way, big enough for us to walk into the deconstructed space. Perhaps something of what Derrida wanted us to see is revealed; that is, the writing itself that goes on forever as *ecriture*. No wonder that he turned his gaze towards the ethics of all this.

Jacques Derrida agrees with Peirce on the idea of *semiosis*.[19] As the saying goes, behind the text, there is only another text. This alleged anti-humanism does not want to stop the movement of semiosis by referring to a static *ens reale*. What became of semiological structure after deconstruction? The answer is given by Richard Rorty, famous for his conversationalist and anti-representationalist philosophy. It becomes, like philosophy in general, a genre within literature. That is, art.[20]

Tristan Hamel
Looking for Risto

Tristan Hamel initiates a project that includes both physical work and theoretical efforts. The project lasts for several weeks and should be seen as a whole. It includes not only the performative high point, a two-week journey on a self-made raft on the Saimaa, the Lake District of Finland, during the summer of 2012, but also diary-based documents, reproductions and plans, together with a post-travel exhibition at the Lume gallery, Aalto University, in Helsinki. All this is spread out both in his thesis work and online.

Hamel discusses the character of environmental art as an example throughout the thesis work, furnishing his work with a rich background of contexts, reflected in the chapters of the text, such as identity, the notion of nature, cosmopolitanism and engagement – and Finland.

If art has become communication, taking quite a few steps out of the modernist and expressionist stance, we must accept that art projects are often multimedia work using various media, including textual elements – and become a body of illustrated and recorded books and video clips based on performative and installatory constructs. We have to accept all this as parts of the artwork, or we do not have a full description of the genre at all.

Hamel argues for a holistic multimedia view of the work of art, at the core of which is, in his case, a strong bent for the experience that can only be had in engagement with nature in practice. This means a change of ordinary adopted routines in the use of time and space, notions of speed, and bodily exposure to the use of muscle power and tools for crafting one's survival in the wild. On top of this matured personality, Hamel explicitly adds travel hardship and its impact, and resistance (weather conditions, distances and time) of the physical environment, all the experiences gathered from the endurance of the self-induced hardship.

In the end, Tristan Hamel burned his Risto, a straw man that remained as theoretical as any philosophical straw man, at a final ritual ending his travels. The dialog that Tristan Hamel had with Risto, his potential alter ego, lives on as a story. This is the fate of most art. The rest goes the same way as Risto. It decays and fades away, having had a temporary shelter in some place, for some duration of time. Hamel proposes that there is no final obstacle for anyone to appropriate a new identity. It only needs engagement in the environment to which one is attracted. The rest comes with our being humans with a past that can be moved around as fragments of a narrative – if we care to tell others about it.

PAIKKA

Back to the real (in theory)

The "public" in environmental art points to a paradox of the modernist
notion of a work of art. Roel Meijs takes his point of departure from this
deconstructionist concept of the (former essential and modernist) work of art,
and, as it were, introduces the real world into the narrative, while the (former
modernist and sacred space-cum-artefacts) furniture of art commences to
vanish into oblivion. Björn Lindström and Tristan Hamel try to introduce
a post-deconstructivist, hence a post-mortem stage, in terms of modernism
- as postmodernism must be omitted here.[21] The remnants of the position
as *flaneur*, in Helsinki (Lindström), as well as the remnants of the casual
(hence modern?) tourist or traveler (Hamel) must be considered in terms
of *in memoriam* (of modern art). But these *in memoriams*, in turn, need
new constructions and buildings for another reason. Björn Lindström and
Tristan Hamel extend their projects into a vehicle for the search for a healing
process, a new identity. This is art as service design for just one individual
at a time.

VAI

Finally, Kaisa Salmi steps outside the rhetoric of *oratio obliqua* altogether.
Her thesis work, *Plastic Avalanche*, has a straightforward story behind it, told
by herself. One morning at the kitchen table, having breakfast, Salmi realizes
that we really use too much plastic. Hence, Salmi dumps a giant load of plastic
trash on the main bus-station square (Kamppi), in order to say what she thinks.
This is a demonstration without having to gather a mass of people demonstrating
on the street about it, with their written signs swaying in the air. The work of
Kaisa Salmi, the *Plastic Avalanche*, is direct speech, a demonstration without
aesthetics.[22] There is hardly any order, any contrast, any construction.
The novella in which this line of direct speech is uttered, is the symbolical
context of art. This is what remains of art in her work, a symbolical context,
without which function Salmi would have been heavily fined for littering
public space.

TILA

Admittedly, there is some variation within the perimeters of the plastic
dump by Salmi. But is it composition? Less than a dynamic balance, as
a constructivist work of art should sustain, the plastic is modulated in two
ways, as transportable bulk loads on pallets and as scattered stuff.

Organized by the city, youth take part in workshops to extract particular
stuff and compose their findings, colorful objects, mostly toys and figurines
of kitsch with paraphernalia of mass consumption. This is a great analogy
to kitchen sink painting, non-representatively present. Not the image, but
out of the samples of the real plastic recycled into art form, the kitchen sink
gutter system.

Temporary Monument of Place
2008, Helsinki, Finland

Risto and raft 2012, Saimaa, Finland

Raft 2012, Saimaa, Finland

PAIKKA

And the topic of functionality?

Progressive and economic interests intertwine, emerge and surge in relation to context, production, rhetoric and visual form. At the start (p.4), distinctions by Miwon Kwon help in classifying environmental installations as to a critical idea, in the first two groupings stressing the media situation, while the artwork of the third group (art in public interest) leaves spatial connotations in peace, favoring the segments of reception and use of the project. Kwon treats the overall development on a descending scale of object-orientedness, with an ascending note of "more site-conscious" work. This is in line with the growing element of interaction with not only the environment, but with the living public, clients, co-workers and community.

The Finnish degree works show up in a later stage of the picture painted above, but with a few notches toward working solo, as it were, using the opportunity of an environmental art project to learn something new about themselves, with the exception of, exactly, those projects using the urban space, not private seaside and lake districts.

James Meyer (Meyer 2000, pp. 23–37) defines site-specific art in his survey using two notions, discussing the "literal" and the "functional" site.[23] About the former kind, Meyer states: *The work's formal outcome is thus determined by a physical place, by an understanding of the place as actual .... Reflecting a perception of the site as unique, the work is itself `unique.* Meyer adds that this amounts to a kind of a monument *for* the place. While continuing with Serra's *Tilted Arc* [24] as such a work, literal dominants of the site-specific artworks, where the artist either brings something of a plug-in or addition to the given, are certainly well exemplified in minimalist and assemblage work.[25] This depends on whether we accept the context of, say, art, nature, or humanity, brought in to surround the momentum of "presence" that the site-specificity, by its sheer dimension and immensity, can do for us. Is it not something of this kind of reaching for a sublime that the white cube aesthetics want to emulate?

Meyer tries to override the literal work with a confusing definition of more recent work as defining *a functional site* that *may or may not incorporate a physical place.* But, he continues, the statement of the new kinds of site-specific works, however wide and varied, is a good description of contemporary artwork in general: *Instead, it is a process, an operation occurring between sites, a mapping of institutional and textual filiations and the bodies that move between them... and ... the functional work refuses the intransigence of literal site specificity. It is a temporary thing, a movement, a chain of meanings....*[26]

Such a distinction as Meyer makes seems to separate literality and functionality completely from each other. We should see it rather as relations of dominants and "accents", as it were, both as to what the artist fixes onto and as to how the conditions for using it are available. Singularity and process is not a dichotomy but a compound, depending on the nature of our interest and passion (textual or not) and embodied perception. We end, therefore, with interpreting differing dominants within a large repertoire of responses. In particular, the two descriptions by Meyer are helpful in dividing our attention to site-specific art in relation to two lines of modernist thinking (and kinds of works) running their course. One discourse makes Post-Painterly Abstraction, feeding into Minimalism (the Greenbergian – Fried discourse). A second consists of a more sociological and playful-cum-political nature (the Pop Art and Conceptual Art discourse) from Art and Language, Fluxus, Situationism, and Structuralism to Deconstruction.

Environmental art must be seen, in effect, as the heir of at least two diverging discourses discussing the understanding, means and tasks of art, as mentioned above. Among other things, these two discourses hardly overlap in their ideas on truth and objectivity. Still, the road of deconstruction can be mirrored in both. In the physical tradition of minimalism (and "phenomenology" of form) that became site-specific art; what was deconstructed was the art object as to its materials and sites, uprooted from its position within a dominant modern art space. In the visual conceptualism, be it ironic or analytical – which do not have to exclude each other – deconstruction shows as parallel movements within a visual body of ready-mades. Urban and cultural iconography design architectural surfaces that used to be billboards for advertisements. Adorno tells us, however, that nothing has changed.

Richard Rorty stressed the futility of reaching for a representation mirroring reality. Meaning will be created as fallible steps in order to survive, prosper by negotiating together in a community, much in the way we grope around in darkness, considering the force of both ethnocentrism and solipsism. To put it briefly, the aforementioned dumps language, philosophical or other-wise, from the start in the jar of fiction.

Rhetoric must not need to be mere conversationalist to be ethical. Examples clear enough to stop us require that we must encounter, confront, meet and bump into similar chunks and hard facts to ourselves. Rhetoric is physical from the start. Communication only has to return to its source, the body and its environment. What can be more or less avant-garde than this? Adorno did not foresee the passing of art as something that should happen perforce without its political and revolutionary momentum lost. He seems to believe in a complete unity of form and meaning, or, then, the non-conformist thing to do was to abstract oneself out of the human equation into something higher. Even this belief of Adorno, which is my intuition, does not have to be lost. A perpetually

PAIKKA

changing rhetoric may be my stake here, if only for the arbitrariness of language. When art practices melt together with abductive and intuitive research and public design, we need a fair share of goodwill spelled out as later modes of the culture industry. At this stage, Björn Lindström, Roel Meijs, Tristan Hamel and Kaisa Salmi give us the impression of going upstream to some unknown source, or at least holding their breath before the flushing sound.

The confusion hinted at in the beginning of my exposition belongs to the result of an educational "environmental" change, while some local resistance points in directions elsewhere, as it were, in the flowing stream of a vortex, at one spot at a time. The history and possibilities of contemporary art practices to be continued in the evolving HE environment of Aalto University are both rewritten and profiled anew. Any public artwork must be applied to its environment and become another kind of environment.

The crucial division as to meaning and importance between temporary and permanent work has not been dealt with here. I have chosen to highlight temporary work in order to emphasize the backdrop, the source of creative rhetoric still a foundation for contemporary visual work. This applies to art in its entirety, displaced according to functional differences of sites of performance: the gallery, the museum, the street, the forest, wilderness. A broad variety of what media allow us to do has effects on the scale and nature of the artwork. Communication needs language. Language is a meeting point of different elements. The meeting point may be fragile, temporary, or stable for a long time, and may involve numerous actors, many of which are of non-human environment, bits and pieces of the world we call media, text, non-Aristotelian *substance* of signs and signature.[27]

A fair portion of public art belongs safely, for most of us, within the cozy industry of culture that Adorno saw embodying Enlightenment as Illusion. For environmental art to show the other exit door - to exit art - as safe for Adorno and for us, seems still rather far-fetched an idea. Considering the energy needed to make a communion between art and a just and good living, this implies only a few of us.

VAI

TILA

Epilogue

Peirce did not define quality as a fully discursive representation of something.
For us, quality can be seen on a scale of functionality for allowed purposes of
projects, whatever their position in the world. Perhaps it started with form and
function, with the idea of design. Scientific and artistic quality are embedded in
our testing the feasibility of our purposes within the professional fields, which
change according to purposes that are given space, time and money. For Peirce,
quality was something of a pure feeling, in no position to make any necessary
true statements and testimonies about reality, but possibly a starting point for
an experiment on the virtual and/or material that, with collateral experience,
might lead to something else, rational acts and habits, or inventions. We need
the mediations of signs that suggest to us a possible option determined by
earlier experience. If art is to be seen as fully functional as to its role and utility
in communication, it must in effect be a habit among others, conforming to
dominant practices in the community of others.

PLACE

OR

SPACE

BIBLIOGRAPHY

Adorno, Theodor W. 2001. *Culture Industry Reconsidered, in The Culture Industry, Selected Essays on mass culture.* Edited and with an introduction by J.M. Bernstein, London & New York, Routledge Classics.

Adorno, Theodor W. 1999.*Aesthetic Theory,* Minneapolis, University of Minnesota Press. Translated, edited and with a translator's introduction by Robert Hullot-Kentor.

Baudrillard, Jean. 1991. *Ekstaasi ja Rivous,* Helsinki, Gaudeamus 1991, Finnish translation of the original by Panu Minkkinen: L'autre par slui-même: Habilitation, 1987.

Bergman, Mats. 2009. *Peirce's Philosophy of Communication,* London and New York, Continuum.

Bois, Yve-Alain and Krauss, Rosalind E. 1997.*Formless: A User's Guide,* New York, Zone Books.

Bourriaud, Nicolas. 2002. *Relational Art from the 1990s to Now.* San Francisco, San Francisco Art Institute, 2002.

Derrida, Jacques. 1981. *Plato's Pharmacy, Dissemination,* trans. Barbara Johnson. London: The Athlone Press, pp. 61-172.

Derrida, Jacques. 1984. *Of Grammatology,* Baltimore, John Hopkins University. Translation from orig. G. Chakravorty Spivak, *De la Grammatologie,* Paris, Les Éditions de Minuit 1967.

Eisenman, Peter. 1982. *Eisenman, Peter, House X,* New York, Rizzoli International Publications, Inc.

Kammen, Michael. 2006.*Visual Shock.* USA: First Vintage Books Edition.

Kwon, Miwon. 2002. *One place after another: site-specific art and local identity,* Massachusetts, MIT Press.

Lucebert. 1974. Poems: De zeer oude zingt in *Verzamelde Gedichten.*

Monestiroli, Antonio. 2005.*The Metope and the Triglyph, Nine lectures in architecture,* Amsterdam, SUN Publishers.

Peirce, Charles Sanders. 1931/1958. *Collected Papers* [CP]. Hartshorne, Charles and Weiss, Paul [eds.] 1931-1935; Burks, Arthur W. [ed.] 1958. Cambridge, Mass. Harvard University Press.

Plato. *Faidros,* 257c-279c, Teokset. 3.osa. Finnish translation by Marja Itkonen-Kaila [et al.], Helsinki, Otava 1979.

Rorty, Richard. 1999. *Text and Lumps,* in Rorty, Richard, *Objectivity, Relativism and Truth,* New York,

Cambridge University Press, pp. 78-92.

Rorty, Richard. 1979. *Philosophy and the Mirror of Nature,* Princeton, Princeton University Press.

Saussure, De Ferdinand. 1989. *Course in General Linguistics,* La Salle, IL, Open Court Classics. Translation from the orig. Roy Harris: *Cours de linguistique générale,* Paris, Editions Payot, 1972/1916.

Suderburg, Erika [ed.]. 2000. *Space, Site, Intervention, Situating Installation Art.* Minneapolis, University of Minnesota Press.

Virilio, Paul. 1997. *Open Sky.* Translation Julia Rose: orig. *Vitesse de libération,* London, Verso,

Weckman, Jan Kenneth. 2013.*Flux Aura as Functional Text,* Turku, in Ruohonen, Johanna and Kihlman, Asta [eds.], *Machineries of Public Art From Durable to Transient, from Site-bound to Mobile,* Turku, UTUkirjat University of Turku.

ACCESSED ON-LINE:
Order of appearance

Kwon, Miwon. 2002 www.eipcp.net/transversal/ 0102/kwon/en *Public Art and Urban Identities,* in Transversal, pre-public 1/2002. EIPCP, European Institute for Progressive Cultural Policies. Originally published with the title 'For Hamburg: Public Art and Urban Identities', in Public Art is Everywhere, pp. 97-109. Hamburg: Kulturbehörde, Hamburg, 1997

Hall, Stuart. *Race as Floating Signifier,* video lecture YouTube www.caffeinesparks. blogspot.fi/2007/08/race-floating-signifier. html. Accessed.

Hyvönen, Helena Dean of School of Arts, Design and Architecture, Aalto University in the Finnish Broadcast News, Yle Radio, url: www.yle.fi/uutiset/kriteerit_kertovat_ mika_on_hyvaa_taidetta/6654201. Retrieved 11.11.2013.

ten Hoope, Dave Peter Eisenman - *Between method and madness,* retrieved 13.11.2013 from url: www.scribd.com/nidhi_sharma_48. Author is Dave ten Hoope, www.davetenhoope. com/index.html, retrieved 13.11.2013.

Eisenman, Peter www.en.wikipedia.org/wiki/ Peter_D._Eisenman [retrieved 24.11.2013].

Eliasson, Olafur www.olafureliasson.net [retrieved 24.11.2013].

Tschumi, Bernard www.villette.com [retrieved 24.11.2013].

REFERENCES

[1] Weckman Jan Kenneth, *Flux Aura as Functional Text,* Turku, in Ruohonen, Johanna and Kihlman, Asta [eds.], *Machineries of Public Art From Durable to Transient, from Site-bound to Mobile,* Turku, UTUkirjat University of Turku 2013

[2] Theodor W. Adorno, *Culture Industry reconsidered,* an essay in: Adorno, Theodor: *Culture Industry, Selected Essays on Mass Culture* [edited and with an introduction by J.M. Bernstein], London and New York, Routledge Classics 2001, p. 100.

[3] Baudrillard concerning public rhetoric and power, in my opinion, as the development of culture [industry] as a state where *floating signifiers* are not determined by any referent, while *signifieds* are torn out of their vertical hiding place from transcendence, onto the table, as it were, which makes postmodernity a site of obscenity. Who says that institutions of education can avoid this *status interruptus* of critical stance to society and ethics? The metaphor of the binary sign may be used in other ways, as well. In my case, the binary sign acts as a metaphor of the public work of art, where *semiosis* is constructed, each time, by the public, the passers-by, as it were, in the public studio of production of meaning. The artist furnishes the signifiers and spectators with their signifieds, voilà, complete sign, every time! *Pace* Peirce and his notion of semiosis, this was not the way Saussure intended his terminology to be used, though. But who cares? Cf. Baudrillard, Jean, *Ekstaasi ja Rivous,* Helsinki, Gaudeamus 1991 [orig.: *L'autre par lui-même: Habilitation,* 1987. Stuart Hall discusses race as a floating signifier. Use the word art instead, and listen, see url: www.caffeinesparks.blogspot.fi/2007/08/race-floating-signifier.html. Retrieval 25.11.2013.

[4] Dean of School of Arts, Design and Architecture, Aalto University in the Finnish Broadcast News, Yle Radio, url: www.yle.fi/uutiset/kriteerit_kertovat_mika_on_hyvaa_taidetta/6654201. Retrieved 11.11.2013.

[5] As Plato tells us, *the pharmakon* being writing [a form of language] that distances itself from its creator and may turn into poison for a reader too far away to understand the intentions of the writer. See Plato's Phaedrus 257c-279c. Needless to say, I am not expounding on the wider notion of *pharmakon* by Jacques Derrida for his own philosophical purposes. See Derrida 1981, pp. 61-172.

[6] My whole approach could well be described as a consequence of trying to envisage the ways a modernist heritage can be displaced within cultural industry. My attitude is, however, while posing as the enemy of autonomous art, to be residing in ever so many relations of public communication, more out of a curiosity of the outcome than despair on behalf of Adorno.

[7] There are several interesting solutions of mining art-based practices from a fuzzy storage of contemporary art that beg the question, how to adjust art into societal design and service formats while advancing towards community art and "relational aesthetics" [Bourriaud 2002]. I will here, however, restrict myself to those topics revealed in the discussion on public art.

[8] Modernism, at least in the Finnish view, seems to predominantly signify the non-pictorial, non-representational and abstract- cum-minimalist version of mainly painting and sculpture, however, by-passing well-known ideological and narrative themes behind the work of, say, Kandinsky, Mondrian and the New York School of Painting - including modern expressionism and surrealism, among other shadowy areas. For reasons difficult to evoke, conceptualism and avant-garde, as a modernist form of practice, seem compressed into an ahistorical package within contemporary art, professing to stand alone without "function", which belongs to design and architecture. For the Finnish art scene, everything is contemporary outside abstract art.

[9] I am simplifying the ambivalence and dynamics Adorno opens for us to embrace: the complexity of modern art as to its double position within cultural and technological modernity: *Art keeps itself alive through its social force*

of resistance; unless it reifies itself, it becomes a commodity [Adorno, 1999, p. 226]. The paradox of this sentence is staggering in relation to voiced intentions in contemporary art as to its essential immateriality. Here, one has, as I do, to steer away from Adorno in accepting art as communication. The next sentence, namely, reveals that Adorno excludes communication as a certain form of resistance that, however, includes an "immanent" aesthetics: *Its contribution to society is not communication with it but rather something extremely mediated: It is resistance in which, by virtue of inner-aesthetic development, social development is reproduced without being imitated.*

10 See Peirce on *Communicational interpretants,* describing a phase of the signifying process shared by speaker and listener, as a general example of communication, in Bergman, 2009, p. 124. Admittedly, the reference could be much expanded so as to open up the view of mutual sharing of objects for significance and interpretation, a view on the triadic sign concept and semiosis by Charles Sanders Peirce, one of the two modern pioneers of semiotics.

11 Here, as in an earlier text of mine, referred to in the title, I do rely on a shorter and earlier online text by Kwon in terms of grouping the development into suitable boxes or subtitles: Kwon, Miwon. 2002. *Public Art and Urban Identities in Transversal, pre_public 1/2002.* EIPCP, European Institute for Progressive Cultural Policies. Originally published with the title *For Hamburg: Public Art and Urban Identities,* in Public Art is Everywhere, pp. 97-109. Hamburg: Kulturbehörde Hamburg, 1997. Here from url:www.eipcp.net/transversal/0102/kwon/en. Accessed October 10, 2012.

12 Favoring a continuation of the logic of the modern, the new is simultaneously a continuation of the old. What come to mind in such a thought pertaining to scale are a number of things, from the neo-conservatism in postmodernist movements such as YBA, or the museal parallell of Tate Modern and eerie monuments by Antony Gormley.

13 Dewey, John, *Art as Experience,* New York, Paragon Books 1979

14 A former slaughterhouse area in Paris became an urban park with an architectural complex for music, and a national science and technology museum. Commencing with an international architectural competition with 460 teams from 41 countries, it was won by the French architect Bernard Tschumi in 1983. The development was completed in 2000. The Tschumi project became famous for its "deconstructive" manner of planning devices for the park as open to public, with its "non-functional" sites and constructions. See url: www.villette.com [retrieved 24.11.2013]. To me, Bernard Tschumi embodies, as an architect, the shift from modernist sculpture gone wild and big within architecture. The passion of this artistic format can be glimpsed from url: www.tschumi.com [retrieved 24.11.2013]. Comparably minor but more poetic solutions within the same genre, spatial art in conjunction with architecture, realized as formal plug-ins with an extensive theoretical fiction behind it, can be seen in Olafur Eliasson's work designed in his Institute für Raum-experimente, url: www.olafureliasson.net [retrieved 24.11.2013]. The area between installation work and architecture is a dominant line of direction, for some, out of the world of art into the world of design. Questions on functionality and character, be it visual, textual, interactive, social, public and economic remain the same. The virtual power games in society are not restricted according to discursive notions.

15 Monestiroli, Antonio, *The Metope and the Triglyph,* Nine lectures in architecture, Amsterdam, SUN Publishers, 2005 p. 25.

16 Eisenman, Peter, House X, New York, Rizzoli International Publications, Inc., 1982 p. 8.

17 Or, perhaps, exactly the refusal to plan ahead reads as art? In such a rhetorical resistance, the keen insight about the context of art already in place, as we undergo this feeling of freedom of art, something clearly has to be feigned like in a child´s play.

[18] See Peter Eisenman - *Between Method and Madness,* retrieved 13.11.2013 from url: www.scribd.com/nidhi _sharma_48. Author is Dave ten Hoope, www.davetenhoope.com/index.html, retrieved 13.11.2013. This is not an Aalto University thesis work, and was found in my search for architectural examples of discussion on the notions of deconstruction.

[19] In binary terms of semiology, the signifier becomes the signified and vice versa in a possibly endless chain of signs. The reference Derrida uses in his work, *Of Grammatology,* p. 50, refers to Peirce and his *Collected Papers* [CP] 2.303. Cf. Bergman discussing the difference between *unlimited semiosis,* a notion coined by Umberto Eco [1978] and the Peircean semiosis, see Bergman, 2009, p. 118. This conflict between idealism and pragmatism emulates [and becomes an icon in my mind for] the options for architecture and art, either as objects and signs of an ideal world separated from what goes on in concrete reality, as when we gasp at the urban landscapes as figments of a greater mind - from Sullivan to Eisenman and Tschumi - or the artist in the era of sculpture. In short, there is no categorical interruption between 3D architecture and 3D sculpture. The former is just bigger and more critical as to safety, sustainability, and use-value than the artwork. Here, in between, we find something other than sculpture: environmental art that wants to avoid the fate of public design - or becoming *"hostile to humanity",* as the saying goes in relation to Peter Eisenman's allegedly first deconstructive piece of architecture. See url: www.en.wikipedia.org/wiki/ Peter_D._Eisenman [retrieved 24.11.2013]

[20] See Rorty, Richard, *Philosophy and the Mirror of Nature,* Princeton, Princeton University Press 1979. The suggestion of an affinity between literature as a fictional genre and philosophy stems from Rorty's thesis that we should drop useless strivings in philosophy, like that exemplified in Wittgenstein's early work, *Tractatus,* which emphasizes the possibility to create a mirror-like representation of the world, given the cleaning work to be done to language,

and resolved within a system of representations that connects language and the "lumps" and the world [the latter wording from an oppositional essay on representationalism by Rorty]. Cf Rorty, Richard, *Text and Lumps,* in Rorty, 1999, pp. 78-92.

[21] I refuse to use the term post-postmodern.

[22] On art objects, and objects arriving into art through rewritten points of view, see Bois, Yves-Alain and Krauss, Rosalind, *Formless: A User's Guide,* New York, Zone Books, 1997, pp. 245-252. The work of Kaisa Salmi, *Plastic Avalanche* might awaken a certain dispute of interpretation between *l'informe* and *abject.* The object should, as it were, change into another kind of object. But, one asks, to what end? Obviously, surrounding old objects or yet non-existing ones with a new vocabulary, does produce something, that is, the new vocabulary and more than that, an institutional move, say, art or a new exhibition. If we go with Saussure, close at hand, we also make new objects through new viewpoints [Saussure, 1989 p. 8]. Viewpoints are not only idealist objects of discourse, but concrete events like an exhibition surrounded by speech and writing.

[23] Mayer, James, *The Functional Site; or, The Transformation of Site Specificity,* in Suderburg, Erika [ed.], *Space, Site, Intervention, Situating Installation Art,* Minneapolis, University of Minnesota Press 2000, pp. 23-37

[24] On Richard Serra's *Tilted Arc* and the site as literal and one with the add-ons or changes made by the artist, a very short note, see Miwon Kwon's essay, *One Place After Another,* in Suderburg 2000, p. 39. To those new to the case of the Tilted Arc, it must be added that the steel wall by Richard Serra installed in 1981 at the Foley Federal Plaza in Washington, was removed by court order in 1989. On the debate about the removal, see, for example, Kammen, Michael, *Visual Shock.* United States: First Vintage Books Edition, 2006. Environmental art takes mostly another road, while the urban environment fits the category.

PAIKKA

Some questions on the privacy of the environmental art site could be raised and compared with the semi-public space of the gallery. My examples here do not show any straightforward possibilities in separating urban from other sites *per se*. The difference should be treated as a narrative and thematic ingredient [including the intentions of the artist] in an otherwise pragmatic set-up named art, as what it pertains for the theoretical response is something else in an adjacent institution

VAI

[25] Notwithstanding the question as to what degree, however, literal early earthwork might be considered, when elaborating on their "phenomenological", ecological or other narratives - if the negative dialectics of a pure phenomenological interest could be accepted as a narrative as well. Perhaps in hindsight, it is extremely difficult to separate iconic artworks from their discursive reception and theoretical context, albeit changing and ephemeral, not forgetting the statements of the artists themselves. Kwon [2000, p. 38] considers early earthworks as *"radical displacements"* from the *"uncontaminated and pure idealist space of dominant modernisms"*. I tend to disagree, in favor of an impure displacement with a renewed interest in the *"pure phenomenological space"*

of art. Put otherwise, by renewing media, recurring interests can survive refreshed, in relation, say, to a painting by Ad Reinhardt or Mondrian.

[26] Meyer 2000, p. 25

[27] Here, the term substance is of Saussure [1989, pp. 157, 169], not Aristotle. My reference here is to equate the notion of medium and media with Saussurean substance, which enabled Saussure to delimit the materiality from the sign, and hence, from the system of language. On the question of writing, however, Saussure, stressed its difference from speech, being a separate language. In that, Saussure did not mean the dots on the paper, the physical material, but the system of language "in" writing. On the complexity of such a separation and generally on Saussure's degradation of writing to another, lower level, than "living" speech, see Derrida, who also refers to Plato and Phaedrus 277e, which condemns writing "precisely as play, [*paidia*] and opposes such childishness to the adult gravity [*spoudē*] of speech [Derrida 1984, pp. 50-51, on Saussure, pp. 45- 46.] The agenda of deconstruction as context for the theme on writing by Derrida, within which I've picked my sources, cannot be dealt with here.

TILA

Kaupunki
-interventiot

Urban
Interventions

Intervention 2003, Helsinki, Finland

Intervention 2002, Turku, Finland

Intervention 2002, Helsinki, Finland

Intervention 2002, Turku, Finland

Intervention 2008, Helsinki, Finland

108

Intervention 2001, Helsinki, Finland

Tie / The Road 2002, Espoo, Finland

Intervention 2003, Helsinki, Finland

Art and Energy in the Cityscape

Martti
Hyvönen

Art and Energy
in the Cityscape

To be stable to sit on, a chair needs four legs. The environmental strategy
of Helsingin Energia rests on four pillars; besides the tripod of Sustainable
Development: Economy, Ecology and Social responsibility, we consider also
Culture and History to be necessary for our centenary company to continue
another hundred years. Public acceptance of products and services is, alongside
with competitiveness, a major factor of success. Art is part of good relations with
neighbors and stakeholders, but we definitely do not use it to whitewash our
image. I consider art has a cultural value and a communicative value in itself.

I personally became acquainted with professor Markku Hakuri´s concepts
and practice of environmental art in the turn of the century. Conceptual art
had been one of my favorites as it lends to many interpretations like life itself.
I was very impressed with the work by Roel Meijs' "road in water", white planks
floating in a river in Espoo.

Year 2000 Helsinki was the European Capital of Culture and both
the University of Art and Design Helsinki (UIAH, later on Aalto University)
and Helsingin Energia were engaged in visual and lighting projects. Getting
to know each other, Markku Hakuri and his valuable project secretary Inka
Finell were easy partners in workshops joining art students, energy system
planners and the environmental team of the company. The Outdoor Lighting
Unit illuminated bridges and quaysides and created also light artworks that have
remained in the night cityscape of Helsinki. Head of the unit Olli Markkanen
has since been active and enthusiastic partner in many projects with UIAH.

Visual projects

The Fake Moonlight, 2000

Emanating from the Floating Gardens project of UIAH, Soila Hänninen´s environmental artwork *The Fake Moonlight* has been very successful. The three-meter high specially honed concave disc weighs two tons with support and uses preprogrammed floodlights to give the impression of a second moon in the horizon. Electrical and service technicians help was needed to install, and later to remove and store the artwork. This artwork was meant to be visible on the western shore of Koivusaari island for a year. But as people and the company liked it, it remained there for over five years until the pier lighting was changed.

Together with Soila we have applied and got permits from the Board for the cityscape of Helsinki for a new seaside location for the artwork. We plan to have solar panels to power the floodlights illuminating the disc, like in the case of the real Moon. The concept of a "fake moon" in the horizon has also educative value and thrills the imagination.

Poor Man's Versailles, 2003

Initially, power plant sites were located to the outskirts of the city. The growing city has one by one encircled them with habitation and office buildings, and the number of people walking by and living close has kept increasing.

As the Kellosaari stand-by plant was refurbished, the landscaping of the concrete wall, oil tank and the grounds was decided. A participatory workshop with Markku Hakuri´s students yielded eight proposals that were submitted to the vote of the power plant staff and the neighbors in a local supermarket. The wallpaper-themed paintings and a red tarmac path amongst red cedar plantings by Klaus Aalto was everybody´s favorite. He named the artwork *Poor Man's Versailles*.

The public has liked this environmental artwork, which can be interpreted in many ways. Some have said that the yellow and red flower themes on the tank and walls give a homely impression to immigrant inhabitants of the district. Even a wedding has been organized on the grounds and in the socket of the oil tank.

Passing Energy, 2005–2007

The Passing Energy cooperation project was launched with the Department of Visual Culture. In an international workshop led by Markku Hakuri, students looked at ways of redesigning electricity distribution boxes. The grey metal boxes on city sidewalks go sometimes unnoticed, quite often they tempt to paint graffiti or glue posters on them, and they number over 8000 in Helsinki. At the company we were aware that they do not always embellish the streets although they are necessary to satisfy the rising demand for power in the city.

The students, company staff, city planners and also a distribution box manufacturer picked the most suitable proposals for development. There was one aesthetic redesign of the link box, but it could not yet compete with the much less expensive traditional metal boxes. The other chosen proposals were based in using the boxes as support for pictures and social messages. These boxes have since had much less graffiti and smudge on them than usually. The main reason for the project was not this. Many of us even think that some mess belong to the street view, everything has not to be clinically clean.

Déjà Vu, 2005–2007

For her project in the workshop, student Zeenath Hasan engaged school-children to take a photo of an item or a view from their way to school passing an electricity box. With the pupils she then chose two per school to be enlarged and installed on boxes. All of these children's photos were presented in an exhibition. Quite amazing is that these déjà vu images have been adopted by new generations of school children. On their way to school, the kids keep the plastic cover of the photo clean. A number of the original pictures are still in place almost ten years later.

Street Galleries, 2005–

The distribution box is the final link between the electricity network and the wirings in household, office and shop premises. The box protects the cables and switches inside, and people outside from the currents created by the 400 Volt appliance. The polycarbonate plates onto which the artwork copies are laminated have to be tested fireproof. Skilled electricians install these on the boxes.

The idea to display works of visual art in the open urban environment, and not only inside gallery walls came up from the idea of artist Magdalena Åberg. She regretted that the images in the cityscape are mostly of commercial advertising. During her studies the workshop gave her the opportunity to realize her idea. This project has become a brand in itself, and she has been awarded more than once. Quite remarkable is that at the 2013 Art Helsinki exhibition, the Finnish Art Gallerists' Association allocated Street Galleries the recognition "Art performance of the year".

PAIKKA

In co-operation with the Association of Finnish Printmakers, the first street gallery was opened in 2005 on the link boxes of Museokatu Street. The graphic artworks on about half of the boxes of the residential street are quite unobtrusive which takes passers-by by surprise to discover that they form an exhibition. Over the next years Magdalena and our team choose Eerikinkatu in the center of the city for photographic art, and Fleminginkatu in the bohemian district of Kallio to host a gallery of drawings. From the third year on, the Helsinki Artists´ Association became partner of the project.

Besides giving young artists the opportunity to expose in public, and for a whole year, Magdalena has also chosen a theme for which the applicants can propose their works. The first theme was Impermanence. Then came Man with the intention to convey a more multifaceted vision of corporeality than that of advertising fixated on sex. Health images questioned what is physical health, what is mental health, and what do they mean at different ages, in different cultures? Year 2009 the theme Power came closer to energy issues as people are beginning to understand that power sources are not inexhaustible nor without adverse effects.

VAI

The next year´s theme was boldly Counter-power. Street galleries mean co-operation and compromise with the city´s law and order, and on the other hand, defying it. Later, the issue of Order – Disorder was discussed through the artworks. A very actual theme of 2013, Growth – Degrowth, meaning both aspiration and an organic being, attracted over forty proposals demonstrating the viability of the concept. Six artists were chosen that year.

Although the images laminated on the polycarbonate sheet are copies of original works, they get influences of weather, and sometimes comments of passers-by, becoming artworks in themselves. Also out of concern not to waste precious material, recycling of the plates has begun. They have been exposed in a metro station and people want to buy works that please them.

Once we wondered how many people actually participate in the process of coordinating, planning, fabricating, installing, communicating and organizing the yearly galleries. Like in the end of movies, we put in the Internet a rolling "Also starring" list of names, which counted up to 40 people. Over the years, more than 130 young artists have participated in street galleries.

TILA

Electricity boxes have been used as support for advertising, paintings etc. elsewhere. But giving the opportunity to artists to participate in a communicative project is a quite unique idea. Other cities have since copied it. In one case they were so polite that besides mentioning Magdalena Åberg as the mother of the idea, they also used the same form and font in the name stickers and maps of their street gallery.

The Fake Moonlight 2000, Espoo, Finland

Poor Man's Versailles
2003, Helsinki, Finland

Déjà vu 2005, Helsinki, Finland

Worker's gone 2009, Helsinki, Finland

Energy Pulse 2010, Helsinki, Finland

Nuage vert 2008,
Helsinki, Finland

PAIKKA

VAI

TILA

Art on the Union Line, 2012–2015

The City of Helsinki celebrated its 200 years as capital of Finland in 2012.
The long straight Unioninkatu Street traversing the city from the Observatory
Hill in the south to the Church of Kallio in the north was chosen to symbolize
the matter. Art on the Union Line jubilee exhibition was organized by Magdalena
Åberg, the Helsinki Artists' Association and Helsingin Energia. Helen Networks,
Eltel Networks and Helsinki City Transport Company assisted in the realization
of the gallery.

Contemporary Finnish art from nine renowned artists is showcased on
distribution boxes along the Union Axis. The exhibition takes its themes from
the street's diverse past and present. The axis has been a dividing and at the
same time a uniting line: Union of Finland and Russia in the 19th century, white
and red sides in the Civil War of 1918, churches and the University, businesses
and art galleries.

Art pictures have longed for a place where they can meet the living city,
the public, the people. Even without direct commercial purposes, the friendly
cooperation with artists and the visibility of Helsingin Energia in the streets
affect on what the people think of it.

Cityscape

Being part of the city, having production and distribution in the city, the visual
aspect of power plants, installations and networks has been important to Helsingin
Energia since building of the first Suvilahti steam turbine plant in 1909. It was
designed by architect Selim A. Lindqvist and was Finland's first reinforced
concrete-based building in which architecture undisguisedly supported the
structure. Since then, renowned designers have put their mark on power plants
(e.g. Timo Penttilä, Hanasaari Power Plant), office buildings (e.g. Alvar Aalto:
Sähkötalo Headquarters) or power line pylons (e.g. Antti Nurmesniemi: Antti's
Steps in Töölö).

Antti's Steps, 2003

Against the city center shoreline, five sculptural, bright blue landscape
columns rise out of the sea. The design and execution process of the overhead
power line involved city residents right from the start. This way, approval
and acceptance was gained for the project, which would change the Helsinki
seascape considerably. The name honors the designer Antti Nurmesniemi

who died a few months after the completion of the line. The power links in with the visual form of the line landscape. Afterwards the pylons have been a popular sight for strollers and tourists on the seaside, as well as for TV cameras to illustrate news about energy.

The experience of communication between different disciplines, engineering, art, sociology, and being open to public opinions has since shaped the approach of the Environmental team at Helsingin Energia. Besides technical and economic aspects, also cultural, aesthetic and ethical values should belong to the processes of planning and building the energy infrastructure for the future.

Hanasaari A, the silent and ugly, 2002–2008

The Hanasaari A coal-fired power plant in Helsinki was built at the end of the 1950s. The first large-scale cogeneration plant, producing power and heat in the same process, was technologically very advanced in its time. The technicians were very proud of it: It was like driving a Mercedes. But, with increasing environmental awareness, as the dust emissions were not filtered well enough, the twin smokestacks of Hanasaari A became a symbol of pollution. The worker's were not happy to tell people where they worked. In the late 1990's Hanasaari A was turned into a standby plant and a "culture factory". Helsinki City Council affirmed the resolution to dismantle the already closed power plant in the end of 2006.

As has happened elsewhere, the young generation of visual artists took inspiration of the "silent and ugly" building for various performances and artworks. Thus Hanasaari A became a spontaneous culture factory in the beginning of the 21st century. Photographers, set designers, music video makers and even film directors fell in love with the rough ambience of the big boiler and turbine halls, the jungle of piping and the handcrafted valves and measuring instruments, industrial design of the 1950s. In a way, Hanasaari A was rehabilitated, and the old workers could again be proud of it.

In 2008, Helsingin Energia received a rare industrial heritage award from the Society for the Industrial Heritage. The reason for the society's decision was that the company has handled the demolition of the old Hanasaari A power plant in an exemplary way.

Light and Space, 2007

A workshop of students of Visual Culture illustrates different interpretations of environmental art. Their proposal for illuminating the old Hanasaari A power plant was realized in the winter 2007. For the students, as well for

PAIKKA

Markku Hakuri, climbing on the roof and the gratings of the plant was
a thrilling experience. Green tones were projected on the smokestacks and
the big turbine hall, which, through high windows, was visible to the main
street in Sörnäinen district. All the green lighting was time-to-time flickering.

For most of the passers-by the green lights on the power plant was
just another light show. But youngsters understood the message: Hanasaari A
had been turned into Homer Simpson's unlucky nuclear plant in the popular
TV series.

Hanasaari A, documentary film 2009

The filmmaker Hannes Vartiainen and Pekka Veikkolainen, student of graphic
design at that time, had asked to install a camera on the top of a smokestack
to shoot a sequential still video during the whole demolition process of the
old plant. They also got permission, after thorough safety training, to move
around and film in the building during the dismantlement of the machinery
and installations.

VAI

At the Film Festival of Tampere, the documentary got the Risto Jarva
award, the biggest movie award in Finland. They won also at a festival in Hong
Kong. The jury described the film as a gentle farewell to an era: It combines
live footage, photographs and animation in an accomplished manner, creating a
visually fantastic and touching depiction of the changing cityscape. The tearing
ruthlessness of time is crystallized in images of demolition machines' jaws
sinking into the brick walls of the old power plant.

Worker's gone 2009

An empty ground extends now where the Hanasaari A power plant once
stood. The site waits the construction of residential blocks on the shoreline of
the city. Besides the written, photographic and film material, a sculpture in front
of the still existing Hanasaari B power plant reminds of the industrial history.

TILA

A group of young art and design students from Japan, Spain, France and
Finland had a project "From scrap to environmental art". Markku Hakuri
initiated the workshop in which also the Academy of Fine Arts took part.
Apart from the steel frame of the sculpture, all the material was reshaped
from demolition scarp of the Hanasaari A machinery and piping. The students
devised the objects: tools, overalls, and a helmet to be welded, and made a scale
model. The place of the worker himself has been left empty.

The monument repeats the massive scale of the power plant; it is six
meters high and weighs five tons. Proper strength assessment and welding

had to be done by skilled workers who eagerly participated on this project. Finally, on the pedestal of the sculpture are engraved the names of both the artists Antton Mikkonen, Elena Alonso, Elise Matineau and Jumpei Shimada, and the metal workers Ahto Penne and Hannu Jukarainen. The soul of the project, Antton said: The starting point was to give the scrap a new purpose and at the same time to create a monument as a tribute to the decades of work at the power plant.

One Hundred Years of Energy Constructions in Helsinki, monographs 2005–2012

In view of Helsingin Energia's Centenary celebration in 2009, instead of the usual book on company's administrative, technical and economic history, it was decided to look at the past hundred years through architecture and the place of energy infrastructure in the cityscape. Altogether five monographs were published; four of them written by Laura Aalto and the fifth by Maija Mäki, assisted by the same steering group. The presentable design and layout of the series is by Kari Pilkkakangas.

The first volume of the book series looks at Sähkötalo, serving as Helsingin Energia's headquarters, through Alvar Aalto's eyes. The third volume concentrated on cityscape, power grids and urban lighting. The role of electricity over the years was viewed from the perspective of an individual residential block and its inhabitants. The aesthetic projects Antti´s Steps and Street Galleries were narrated in this volume.

Invisible energy

Man's relationship with energy is a distant one. One only notices energy when it is no longer there. Physically, power consumption precedes production, if only by 0,8 seconds. The energy chain is usually represented from energy sources through production and transmission to consumption. We like to represent the flow the other way round: The level of comfort at our homes and offices determines how much electricity, heating and cooling Megawatts need to be produced. People are not wasting energy on purpose, but, as it is so invisible, inadvertently. Paradoxical as it may sound, Helsingin Energia wants customers to use less power and less heating.

PAIKKA

VAI

TILA

Nuage vert (Green Cloud), 2008

A Paris based couple of artists, Helen Evans and Heiko Hansen presented the Nuage vert concept at the Pixelache festival of Helsinki in 2005. From the Suomenlinna artists' residence they saw the plume of the Salmisaari power plant over the city and found the changing man-made cloud beautiful although representing pollution. Could it convey a message on energy consumption?

Time was needed for the company directors to take an open-minded attitude towards the realization of this unusual artwork, and engineers had to work hard to provide the real-time power data from the complex information systems.

A strong, green laser beam drew the shape of the steam cloud in the sky, detected by a sophisticated thermal camera system. The shape and size of the cloud kept changing according to the power consumption in the district: The less electricity used, the bigger (and more beautiful) the cloud.

Interaction with the local residents was expressed through the Nuage vert. Households were asked to put off the lights some evenings, a great number participated, and, even big businesses in the area wished to join the initiative. The performance lasted one winter week only, but it was very popular, reported on TV and the media, and awarded internationally. Years after people remember the concept of Nuage vert, which is still visible in the Internet.

After Helsinki, Helen and Heiko have struggled to realize a similar communicative project in Paris, on the plumes of a big waste incinerator in Saint-Ouen. A green intervention was realized in 2010, but blocked by local authorities since. The artists mean that the interaction with the cloud is not only a symbolic gesture. On a social level this includes engagement with local people, public authorities and technicians to develop an imaginative language to discuss energy consumption or waste production. An attractive issue has been to discuss whom the cloud of water vapor emanating from the smokestack belongs to. Well, the cloud in the sky belongs to everyone.

Visualization projects

We feel that graphs or even simple traffic lights do not convey the energy saving message very attractively. Further visualization projects are ongoing with artists, city planners and sociologists. Power Flower, visual artist Andy Best's sketch of a kinetic sculpture reflecting both power and heat consumption, the flowers withering with increasing demand, and vice versa, got realized to two meter scale model and a video presentation in 2009. The fantasized 20 meter high kinetic sculpture on the Kamppi Square is still on hold.

Information visualization designer Miska Knapek, also a former student, is very clever in transforming digital data into artworks. On the occasion of

Earth Hour 2010 he projected *Energy Pulse* on the facade of the National Theatre. Colored balloons ran up the wall in the rhythm of power and heat consumption.

The Alppila peak load heating plant was refurbished in 2011. The particular double concave smokestack is visible from the city center over the inner bay Töölönlahti. With the designer Päivi Raivio from UIAH we decided to paint the stack with energy saving LED lighting. The evenly changing nine colors are nice to see as such, but the hidden message is that the color reflects district heating Megawatts on that hour comparing to the average of past years at the same temperature. The issue of open-source data is to be considered also from the intimacy point of view: whom belong the kWh readings, and what do they unveil? The invisible kWhs should be visualized in a symbolic and tempting way.

Epilogue

One central objective of Helsingin Energia's interest group work is to ensure the operational preconditions in its energy supply areas – power plants, substations, heating plants, multi-utility tunnels, distribution networks – in the increasingly dense urban structure. Industry is also a part of urban landscape.

The lively and open communication in Markku Hakuri´s workshops has strengthened my belief that trust, freedom and tolerance are essential for new and creative outcomes of any teamwork. The art projects have shown that you cannot exactly plan participatory networks in advance; people become stakeholders and partners during the realization of projects. Empowering happens naturally.

The perseverance of artists is often remarkable; they do not resign easily from ideas they believe in. In this cooperation I have been grateful that conscience-sensitive design students and artists have accepted to work together with energy company staff, which, quite understandably, can raise contradictory feelings.

As mentioned in the beginning, I consider environmental art has great communicative value, and it is part of everyday aesthetics and everyday sensations that we need.

Participatory Art and its Space

Polly
Balitro

Participatory Art and its Space

The interactive nature of installation art nowadays in relation to the various spaces where it can be found; from the art museum to the public space, from the public space to the virtual space of the web.

As much as installation art is an artistic genre that depends on its space – being often site-specific and designed to change the perception of an environment – it is also true that it also very much depends on interaction with its audience, whose participation in the artistic practice is becoming more and more important. This kind of contemporary installation art, which we can call interactive and participatory, being so dependent on the reaction of its public, is even more dependent on its space, as it is the latter, in fact, that can greatly influence the mood and the behaviour of the audience. In this article, I am going to discuss the participatory nature of installation art and how a space can determine its success or failure, according to my personal experience both as an artist and as an active spectator of the work of others.

Since Kaprow's Happenings and Environments in the 1960s, the term *installation art* has started to imply a concept that goes way beyond the mere physical action of installing a three-dimensional piece of art in a gallery; installations have, in fact, begun to exist as a function of a specific space.

The artist's idea of leaving behind the gallery, which was becoming too aseptic for his audience to respond to, in favour of a more spontaneous and accessible environment, signals an important moment in the history of installation art: Kaprow recognises that it is time for an art piece to be not only shared, but also experienced by the viewers, who should ultimately become part of the artwork itself. Therefore, it is necessary for installation art to exit those spaces that are officially designated for exhibiting art, and instead to be presented directly to the public in a completely different location.

Taking the art piece away from the gallery and bringing it closer to the people instead was essential to Kaprow: in this way, he was hoping to encourage the audience to take part in the installation; there was not going to be any more distinction between the artist and the viewers, who were becoming an active part of the practice.

Places like conventional museums and galleries instead, because of their structure and rules, created a sort of separation between the art piece and

PAIKKA

the audience, discouraging such interaction, so that the viewers remained merely static spectators. Therefore, the innovation of Happenings and Environments, the interaction between the public and the installation, was largely dependent on the spaces where those Happenings and Environments were taking place: lofts, basements and stores downtown became the ideal spaces to destroy the barriers between the art piece and audience, which were so evident and indestructible in the galleries.

It is easy to see why, in the 1960s, lofts and such spaces, so numerous in the city, were more accessible to the artists and their audience: the artists could utilise those places freely, not afraid of putting together something that would be unacceptable in a gallery environment, and the viewers could step into them spontaneously, even when not strictly connected to the art world per se – and this contributed to bringing in a more varied and different crowd compared to that which usually attended official openings in galleries.

VAI

Nowadays, when the art world is even more deeply connected to everyday life, the artists want to be able to talk and interact with their audience freely and spontaneously. A static installation in a museum, where one needs to pay to have access, has very little significance in the contemporary art world; it may become permanent in that museum's exhibition, giving the artist more respectability and visibility among and compared to his / her colleagues, but does it really give the public a chance to establish a dialogue with the artist?

There are surely artists that, even though exhibiting installations in conventional museums, are still looking for a sort of dialogue with their audience – yet this may be a little less spontaneous than they think. In this regard, I remember being in Kiasma some time last year and coming across a rather spectacular audio installation (*The Murder of Crows* – Janet Cardiff and George Bures Miller) on the top floor. I have always wondered, especially when it comes to audio installations, how the visitor to a museum is supposed to react: are they supposed to move around while listening to it? Are they even allowed to move around? That particular installation, though, did not leave the audience with much choice: we were presented with a neat group of chairs, each one with a pair of headphones. Even though there were various speakers all around the room, I felt somehow like I was supposed to be sitting on a chair and listening through the headphones; not to mention that the presence of the ubiquitous Kiasma museum guards was silently preventing me from moving around. That being said, I still found the audio installation to be particularly intense and engaging, but I was left wondering how it would have felt in a different environment, with fewer restrictions.

TILA

It is true that art museums can be very daunting, at times, especially for the audience.

P
L
A
C
E

O
R

100 Feeders 2012, Helsinki, Finland

S
P
A
C
E

More and more installations these days are therefore taking place outside the restricted environments of art museums; while some artists still favour gallery spaces, others try something different.

When speaking of galleries, there are of course galleries and galleries: contemporary artists, especially independent and emerging ones, seem to prefer the broadest concept of gallery, which in fact delineates an indoor space where it is possible to exhibit art. These kinds of galleries are various and different, as they can be found everywhere around the city – from popular to less popular areas, they can be very tiny, like a simple room with a window onto the street – or very big, like an old factory converted into an exhibition space. Just like Kaprow's downtown lofts, where he held his Happenings, these contemporary galleries are definitely more accessible than an ordinary gallery or museum, both for the artists and the audience.

Of course, when it comes to young, emerging artists, one could argue that the choice of the type of space mostly depends on where they are actually allowed to exhibit their works – permission that may be easier to obtain in a non-conventional gallery. This this very important choice especially depends on the installation itself, and on how the artist intends to relate with the public, and ultimately on what kind of audience they are looking for. Here I am not talking about those installation pieces that are possible to move from one place to another, but instead about those that are strictly thought through for a specific space and a specific audience; an artist has to take into consideration both factors for the purpose of their practice.

When aiming to reach a broader audience than the usual museum and gallery visitors, the artist must consider a different option: the public space – an expression that can include various places that are generally open and accessible to people. Indoor public spaces, such as libraries, schools, railway stations and other buildings that are usually accessed by a large number of people of various ages and different backgrounds, become ideal places for the contemporary artists to install their pieces – they become sort of temporary galleries, without being necessarily related to art: in this way, a much broader audience can become familiar with an art piece in a more spontaneous way and on a daily basis. However, as much as libraries and railway stations are accessible to everyone, they are still indoor spaces and, therefore, present a series of rules and restrictions, such as closing times or rush hours; not to mention that usually someone finds themselves in those places for a specific purpose and has hardly any time to dedicate to the installation there. The installation piece, in this case, becomes what we call a *public art* piece – which needs very little to no interaction at all with the passers-by, but remains static in the space.

For these reasons and others, the most suitable places for participatory installation art are outdoor public spaces such as streets, parks and squares. These spaces are not only accessible literally by anyone, but they are also passing-through spaces where a large number of people are bound to be, sooner or later. When artists decide to present their work in a square, they are almost completely free to act as they wish, as long as it does not harm anyone: there are no closing times and it is not necessary for them to ask for permission for their practice. Moreover, the variety of people that passes through a square is certainly more diverse than that which visits a library, not to mention less silent. The spontaneity of an action that takes place in an outdoor public space really has no equal: on a square, in a park, down the road, there are absolutely no barriers between the artists and the passers-by, and no limitations to their dialogue.

As an artist, I have many times dealt with the choice of presenting my work in a gallery or in a public space, and always, when the work in question was of a participatory art nature, I went for the public space option – as in an outdoor public space. In this regard, I would like to briefly introduce my work *100 Feeders*, which I presented as the art practice for my Master's thesis in Environmental Art in 2012. With this project I wanted to invite my audience to feed birds and reflect on this action as a way to remain in close contact with the natural environment, even when living in an urban one. After preparing 100 bird feeders by hand, using recycled materials, and wondering how to give them to people for the purpose of my research, I finally decided that the best place would be in a public space. I had almost immediately rejected the idea of installing my feeders in a gallery, as I did not think of it as the proper place for them to deliver my message: first of all, works exhibited in a gallery are usually for sale, while my feeders were a gift and an invitation to people to start the action of bird-feeding themselves; secondly, I knew I was going to meet a more varied audience outside the gallery space. That is why I organised my *feeders giveaways* – that was the name that I had given to my action – first in an unconventional gallery, which used to be a laboratory for engineers and remained an unusually neglected space, and secondly, and even more effectively for my purpose, in a market square in the city centre of Helsinki. On both occasions, I could involve a much broader audience in my project than a museum or a conventional gallery would have allowed. Moreover, *100 Feeders* took advantage of another type of space, which I have not yet mentioned in this article, but which was fundamental to the success of the project: the web. Through the Internet, in fact, I had the possibility to reach a worldwide audience and get an incredible amount of feedback, which was very useful for my research.

Needless to say, nowadays the virtual space of the Internet has been gaining more and more importance in our everyday lives. Certainly, if a public space is accessible by a large number of people, the Internet, even if only a virtual space, is accessible by a large number of people at the same time and from all over the world – it is the public space for excellence. If the artists wants to establish a dialogue with their audience, is there anything more ideal than the web? It is a convenient place to introduce a project to the public or even to literally start one, giving the audience the possibility to take part in it and continue their art practice wherever they are.

For these reasons, in my opinion, when it comes to participatory art, in our society the Internet may really be the most effective place to share our practice, as artists, and to access new types of art, as audience members. As contemporary artists, it is our duty to present our art to a broader public, to reach a more varied audience; therefore, we cannot really ignore the Internet, but we should start to utilise it for the purpose of our practice, as another type of public space.

On Environmental Art Making

Dan
Snow

On Environmental Art Making

Doing good to the environment is not humankind's long suit. There are precious few ways for us to interact with our natural surroundings that have a positive impact. That's why it's important to approach the making of art out-of-doors, sideways. It should not be difficult for nature to deflect or absorb the making of art in its realm.

Art is not nature. If it was we wouldn't need to make it because it's already made. Nature is not art. An interpretation or contextualization of nature can be art. Augmenting or aggregating nature, intervening in or interacting with nature are potential ways for nature to become art. Left alone, nature creates itself. It is, perhaps, its own art. But that's not ours to judge because as soon as we do, we turn it into art that's of our own making.

To make a piece of environmental art, begin by resisting, for as long as you possibly can, the urge to even think about making something. Explore. Examine. Extract. Take it all in, including the chaotic, the fractured and the missing bits. To ignore incongruities only perpetuates ignorance. Accepting confusion is the the first step toward clarity. Stand up to preconceptions, and at the same time, stand up for intuition. Ask what's been shown, what's being told, what's the experience of the place.

Nature is full of edges, hard and soft, but we hardly notice the transitions. Along every edge, conductivity is taking place. Conductivity is the most active force of nature. Though invisible, the passing of power is so pervasive and ever present we accept it as a given. In microcosms and macrocosms, alike, where there's an abundance of differences the differences disappear through shared border lines.

Look for resolution in the transition between things. Integrity is fashioned at the edges. For something to have stature it must connect to the surroundings. Background is backbone. Strength begins in the distance and accumulates as it moves, by capillary action, toward the center. Connections may be weakest the further they are away from the center but there they are most plentiful. The center gains its strength by pulling energy from its edges.

The horizon line defines the extent to which an environmental art piece can draw power. Energy flows from the background, is gathered up and expressed. In its turn, the piece becomes a point of emanation on other horizon lines. Art made in, and of, nature borrows and loans in equal measure.

P A I K K A

It gains specificity by being contextualized and offers diversity by upturning natural order.

At the site of a work-to-be, take away an impression. Leave with an understanding that can be turned into the groundwork for how to engaged with the place. Still, don't think about what to make. Ask yourself what materials are available and how they might be manipulated.

A sphere of influences, created by the establishment of limitations, surrounds and protects the process of art making. Confined by self imposed boundaries, the work proceeds with good reason for optimism. The central concern, the choice of art, becomes effortless under the right conditions. When all is in place, the making of the art is nothing more, or less, than the joy of being on earth.

Koli Environmental
Art Workshop June 2007

V A I

The pasture hadn't changed much since the forest was cut and the stones removed from the surface of the ground. Horses continued to feed on the grass that shot up every spring. The collection of stones in the middle of the field were said to have been the foundation of a smithy. No evidence remained of a wood structure or the working of iron on the site. There wasn't even an outline of the foundation walls, the ruin had been so thoroughly trampled down by livestock over the years. The only hint that the stones were once arranged to form an enclosure was the birch tree growing at the center of the heap. It had escaped browse because of the topographical barrier posed by the tumbled stones. The tree's thatch of leaves provided the only patch of shade on the pasture ground. The horses claimed it as their own on sunny summer days.

This was the scene that the ten students encountered when they arrived at the workshop site. They met the farmer and acquainted themselves with the land. Their assignment was to make an environmental art piece using stone from the old foundation. Discussions took place around the evening campfire. They decided that the tree needed better protection from the livestock. Their quest would be to save the tree.

T I L A

The completed work was titled *Birch Fortress*. Once the shape of the work was determined, shifting, lifting and careful placement of stones defined the activities engaged in by the students over the course of four days. The students assembled the stones into a wall that ringed the tree. They practiced the hand-

P L A C E

O
R

S P A C E

Aesthetics of Stone workshop 2007, Koli, Finland

craft of dry stone construction while experiencing a singular place in
a variety of ways.

To the casual observer not much had changed from when the students
arrived at the site to when they left the space. The horses were let back into
the pasture and farm life went on as before. The environment was the same.
What was different was the students. They now had intimate knowledge of
a place on earth because they had briefly, but intently, made it their own
through the making of art.

Birch Fortress
2007, Koli, Finland

Looking at Environments

Kurt
Vanbelleghem

Looking at Environments

Mapping a site — Antwerp, March 2013

In the autumn of 2012 I started working as a curator at St Lucas University College of Art & Design in Antwerp. It is my job to assist our master students in artistic projects outside the curriculum and to develop professional opportunities for our alumni. Besides the fact that I help them with their applications for scholarships, residencies and further studies abroad, I also develop specific curatorial projects in which master students and alumni can participate. Through this approach, my art college wants to narrow the gap between the academic curriculum and the 'real' world. I am there trying to avoid the struggle each student has, once graduated, with that 'what to do next?' question. I work with them as artists and no longer as students; I demand the same commitment and professionalism. I take them out of the relative protective shell formed by the academy and inscribe them in professional artistic networks, on a national and international level.

One of the first projects I developed in my position as curator at St Lucas is 'mapping a site', which took place for the first time during the first ten days of March in 2013. It consisted of a one-week workshop with master students from St Lucas University College of art & Design in Antwerp, from the Master in Environmental Art at Aalto University, Helsinki and from Ringling College of Art & Design, Sarasota, Florida. In total eight artists were participating. As a curator, I deliberately have chosen not to work from within an institution like a museum or a gallery. I always preferred to develop projects in specific social contexts that were representing open-ended questions or challenges. Many of the art projects I curated are investigating real situations and are challenging the meaning of art in a specific given context, and by extension the role of an artist in our society.

The 'mapping a site' project in Antwerp was based on those same criteria. The 'environment' existed of one particular road in the center of Antwerp. Within that stretch of approximately 1000 meters one could find the central bus station, the central train station, our national zoo and several main roads that are connecting the city center with the suburbs. It is a short, strait line on the map, but it is a junction where all different cultures of the world meet and live, it is a meeting place for business, entertainment, and dining. 90% of the people are just passing through this area, from home to work and back. All different means of transport (people walking, cars, bikes, trams and buses) are competing for the little available space. It is a 24 hours area. It is everybody's place in no man's land but also no man's place in everybody's land. It is a place with incredible opportunities ranging from boring to hectic.

The site was definitely challenging enough. In order to address this context, it would require a lot of critical thinking and problem solving skills from the students. It was an environment that also wasn't waiting for us; it didn't welcome art. In order to establish something meaningful in a period of one week, it would demand a lot of communication and social skills.

The eight students started of with a lot of on-site research, observing and mapping the relationship between on the one hand the physical form of the spaces at a collective and at an individual scale and on the other hand the qualities and textures of the daily life and behaviour of the inhabitants. This resulted in the artistic description of eight different dynamics, based on particular observations and then translated into specific happenings and performances.

Charlotte Grandgrainage (BE) focused on *uninhabitable public spaces*. She turned the open space between the sidewalk and a storefront into a living room, decorating it with a sofa, a table, curtains and so on. The 'host' invited the pedestrians to join him at his 'home' for a cup of tea, to sit in his sofa and to have a chat.

Sarah Hendrikcx (BE) relied on *the politics of appropriation* for her installation. She selected several buildings on that road and turned them into 'sculptures'. She attached copper nameplates to each one of the buildings on which one could read exactly the same information as you can find on the labels hanging next to a painting or a sculpture in a museum. Each building was the 'work' of a particular artist, and the information about the specific buildings like the year of construction, height, volume and so on acted as elements of the technical description of the 'artwork'.

Kasia Dybek (FL) dealt with *the invisibility of everything*. During the week, she made sound recordings of everything that happened on that road. She then divided the absurd composition into nine abstract soundtracks and registered them on a cd. On the last day, she set up a little market stall and 'sold' the 'music' for zero euros to the inhabitants of the street.

Salla Salin (FI) worked with the concept of *alienation* to make a link between the boredom of the caged animals in the nearby zoo and the daily routine of the commuters taking everyday the same path to and from their work. Her performance consisted of walking up and down for one hour on the same line, between two imaginary points, on the square in front of the central station.

Mapping the Site workshop 2013,
Eva Betjes, Antwerp, Belgiumt

Mapping the Site workshop 2013,
Eva Betjes, Antwerp, Belgiumt

Mapping the Site workshop 2013,
Charlotte Grandgrainage, Antwerp, Belgium

Harri Piispanen (FI) focused on *the insignificant accidents* that were taking place everyday alongside that road. During the week, he observed several accidents or confrontations and described them very briefly in a short scenario. He printed each of those scenarios on a separate white T-shirt. On the last day of the workshop, he wore all these T-shirts on top of each other and started walking from one side of the road to the other. He stopped at each particular point where one of the accidents had happened and waited until a passer-by stopped to read the text on the T-shirt he was wearing. He then took off the shirt, folded it and gave it as a present to that person.

Karen Arango's (FL) project was about *processing temporary actions*. She started with making photographs of objects in the street that were only very temporarily there, like a bike placed against a shop window, a garbage bag on the sidewalk or a scarf that had fallen on the ground. She then made a second photo of the same location without the object. She printed both images and presented them next to each other on a wooden panel that she left behind on that spot.

Eva Betjes (BE) looked at *the cultural diversity as a unity*. She was particular interested in the representation of the many different cultures and nationalities through the goods that were on sale in the shops on that road. She translated the cultural diversity of these objects in kitschy paintings representing ideal holiday locations and settings and then left these paintings behind next to the shops belonging to those immigrant shopkeepers.

Andrea Koll (BE) worked with the concept of *the external gaze*. She focused on the tourists arriving to Antwerp by train and handed out tourist maps of Antwerp to them. But before she distributed the maps, she made a little alternation to them. She carefully removed the specific location of that road by cutting out a part of the map. Visitors using the map were literally left in the void while trying to orientate themselves in order to get out of that area as fast as possible.

Each of the eight participants of this workshop addressed this particular difficult context in an intelligent way, displaying dynamics one often doesn't notice while looking at an environment. It was my first curatorial project I realized with students and I do hope that in the future we can continue to achieve the same quality and intensity.

3.3.2013 11.06 AM
CARNOTSTRAAT

THREE MEN ARE STANDING
BETWEEN TWO CARS PARKED
ON THE DRIVEWAY

THE SECOND CAR SEEMS TO
HAVE COLLIDED WITH THE
FIRST ONE

THE MEN ARE INSPECTING THE
DAMAGE

ONE OF THEM POINTS OUT A
LARGE DENT IN THE REAR
BUMPER OF THE FIRST CAR

Mapping the Site workshop 2013,
Harri Piispanen, Antwerp, Belgium

Human Ornament

Jan-Erik
Andersson

Human Ornament

I am sitting on a tram on my way from the University of Art and Design
Helsinki to the city centre. I am accompanied by a dozen or so participants on
the *Human Ornament* course, spread among the other passengers. I'm having
trouble keeping my cone-shaped hat on my head, and I can see that some course
participants find it hard not to burst into laughter. The hat and my colourful
tunic – both made of cardboard and fabrics of different colours – atract some
attention.

All course participants – including myself, the head of the course
– are wearing fantastic outfits. It is a lot of fun to observe the students; some
have more experience and enjoy being looked at, but some must overcome
their shyness and find it easier to do things as part of a larger group. The other
passengers also react in different ways: some look at us with open bewilderment,
whereas most try to act normal.

We are on our way to decorate Helsinki with ourselves, as part of a five-
day workshop. The course was inspired by my own interest in the significance
of ornaments in creating a "mental space" for individuals. I believe that we
need stimulation, stories, fantasy. All this can be expressed in ornaments, and if
we take a look at the history of architecture, this element – the artistic element,
if you like – has always been an important part of buildings. That is, until
modernism discarded or changed ornaments into meaningless patterns and
clean, harmless surfaces, which resulted in architecture that I mostly find dull
and evasive.

There are such houses on our way to the city centre. We get off the
tram just before Hakaniemi market place, where there are a number of grey,
unornamented façades. My idea is that we first assume various expressive poses
against the said façades, and these are photographed by a photographer. During
the second part of the course, the students use these digital images and use their
expressions to develop patterns that cover the entire façade.

By wearing these clothes and physically moving in the urban environment,
the students become more sensitive to how the places and buildings "feel",
instead of observing them as aesthetic objects from a distance. It is impossible
to be anonymous, to slip away: we are being looked at just like real, static
ornaments, and we must learn to be proud of this.

Human Ornament workshop
2007, Helsinki, Finland

By pressing myself against the facade, I somehow sense that the buildings are also organisms of a sort. They enclose us, provide us with warmth and shelter. In my opinion, they are not merely a background for life, as so much of the contemporary philosophy of architecture wants us to believe. No: they are – or used to be – also able to create life and facilitate human encounters. In order to act as this kind of catalyst for communication, it is by no means unimportant what our environment looks like. By turning ourselves into ornaments decorating buildings, we show how human life in the form of what we call culture should also penetrate buildings. The ornament represents life, as it were.

The most fun part of this kind of course is that it is very much open for improvisation. I realise quite soon that we can make use of the communal balconies in the block of flats. These were commonplace before balconies became a standard element in individual flats. The students show more and more courage, and soon we manage to take a photo with students posing on every shared balcony of a building simultaneously. Balconies can be used to display each resident's aesthetic views, which reminds me of Friedensreich Hundertwasser's thesis "arm's right". This entails each resident of a block of flats having the right to aesthetically modify the area of the façade they can reach from their window.

In the afternoon, we are inspired to invade a concrete complex by the waterfront; this is by no means a concrete hell, rather a luxurious residential block where quite a few influential figures live. We also spot some attempts to decorate the concrete. But still, it is cold and dead. The sheer scale makes us feel like minuscule spots of colour. But the next day, the computers save us, and the resulting montage shows how you can use simple methods during the construction phase to provide buildings with a touch of life.

Course programme:

DAY 1 We start the course with a lecture on the theory of ornamentation. In the afternoon, we visit a fabric shop where the students can pick any fabrics they like. In this way, we kick off the course by doing something that is pure fun together, no work as yet! We hang around as a group in the city, which is a good introduction for the later performance. In the fabric shop, the students (and I) compare different fabrics, pose in front of the mirror, and give comments. What a fine collective experience.

DAY 2 We start with a lecture on the theory of ornamentation. Then we begin to create outfits and hats with cardboard, scissors, glue and needles. When we are finished, we photograph everyone in various poses in front of a white wall, in order to create material for later Photoshop montages.

DAY 3 Performance in two places in central Helsinki. Because I am also participating in the performance in the capacity of the course leader, we need another photographer to shoot us. I think that my personal participation may provide the students with additional motivation to take the plunge. I also find it rewarding to be part of the group: an experience that I will never forget.

DAY 4 The students use Photoshop in the computer lab of the University of Art and Design Helsinki, combining the Day 2 interior poses with photos taken outside during the performance on Day 3. They also use photos of the other participants, which makes the whole project more interesting.

DAY 5 The images are printed and attached on foam board to create a small exhibition for other students and teachers at the school. Creating the exhibition is important, because it provides us with an opportunity to focus on reflecting on what we have been doing.

Ihmisornamentti / Human Ornament workshop 2007, Helsinki, Finland

A place for Miracles

Ossi Naukkarinen

A place for Miracles

*At the end of a faded day, I land on an imitation leather sofa in
a clinical office room, like a leaf falling from a tree. I am cooked
in the stuffy air. Markku and I are trying to get into the swing of
things, planning a course for the coming spring and discussing issues
that some of the students are struggling with in their studies. We go
through the motions of wondering about the lack of money and time,
as we have all become accustomed to doing.*

I would not, however, like to be anywhere else, because this is where miracles
will, again, start to happen. Gradually, from the greyness, colours appear, plants
sprout out of the concrete, human and animal voices are heard from among
the administrative jargon, stuffiness gives way to freshness. Straight lines branch
off, statistics start singing.

∗∗∗

The places that are important and full of meaning are always those in which
something exceptional has happened or is just happening. Something that
leaves a lasting mark, good or bad. A mark etched by an intense sense of living.
A calm or a storm drawn by a giant hand or an echo of eternity.

There is no limit to where these places of power can be found: at home,
in the forests, streets, parks, restaurants, sports arenas, cars, anywhere, even
in the workplace. They are places of importance, places of horror, places
of experience, and we all have our own. Small, large, permanent, variable;
concentrations, excavations, points of the sharpest needles.

Some important places were not created by anyone and nor are they
under anyone's control, they just emerged: natural places, entire cities. But
an artist can undertake to create one.

It is the lot of an artist to create places where exceptionality emerges.
No artist can guarantee that they will be successful, because even the best art
can be extinguished by unappreciative audiences. But the artist aims to bring
what is blurry and unnoticeable into burning focus. This will make the place hot;
the artist shapes emotions, tingles your spine, takes your breath away, stings you.

This is one way of making the world a better, more inspiring, important, memorable, cheerful and miraculous place. Not all art does this, but it is one of the reasons why art exists and why it is valuable.

⁖

Thanks to Markku, the workplace seems like *a place*. This is valuable and all too rare. What contributes to this happening? How does a meeting room turn into an oasis?

As an environmental artist, he is supposed to shape his physical environment, and this is indeed what he does. He is expected to know how. He takes colours, shapes, structures, materials, proportions and routes, and coaxes them into being something other than they supposedly were a moment ago. Otherness unfolds in many forms, making the experiencer sense a space in a manner seasoned with vertigo and realisation.

In Markku's case, this means the emergence of his personality, the presentation of his view, scratching at things, a mixture of screaming and whispering. Markku tells stories about himself and the encounters he has had. And when he does this, we are not dealing with just approaching a space in the physical sense, but with all the stories and actions he associates with the space – in the same way as a church building is tied to the weight of an entire religion. If you do not know the stories, the space is not charged in the same way. That is why an artist should use all the means available: music, sounds, odours, flavours, objects and memories. All these define a context for a place: a place for the mind, a cultural and social place, a space, a landscape, a recess, a feeling. A feeling can just as well be a meeting, a painting class or an excursion.

Some of all this is true, some is something else. What this 'else' is – a dream, lie, belief, joke, fear – is for each experiencer to find out. As is what it means to 'be true'.

Artists can achieve all this with their work, and they can also, through their example, teach what they know to other people, students and colleagues. Markku has done this, too, and he probably would not know how not to. All places teach us something, if we are willing to receive it. At the same time, they hide and make us forget something else; something that we can no longer remember or capture.

⁖

The places that Markku has conjured up produce rippling effects, one of which is me writing this text. Normally, I construct research articles, academic prose that is bound by strict traditions and serious guidelines. I like that, too, but it is very different. This is freer and more playful, more open, and, evidently, more digressive. However, even a text like this is rooted in places and spaces that I carry with me, even if a particular physical place that served as its starting point no longer exists. As the saying goes: you can take a person out of a place, but you cannot take the place out of the person, because places are in the mind, and persistently so.

I can no longer walk into the room with the imitation leather sofa, but I can fly there. If the rules appear to be too strict, you can escape into spaces of words and ideas. Or rather, you can escape through them, because they serve as holes into other realities. I hope everyone has them, although perhaps not everyone misses them. I would hope to see others enjoy the possibility of being transported in this way.

Can I personally create these parallel domains? Even just for someone, sometimes? I do not know, but certainly not by using the same media as Markku. My medium is not visual, physical spaces but words, linguistic acts. Machines made up of letters, syllables, words, sentences and storylines that conjure up a screen of smoke, on which images inspired by that moment are reflected from the eyes of the recipients.

∗

Places do not just exist. Places are constantly being created. We all have a role to play in how they are created and how they turn out, and in whether just one or several are created at the same time.

I know it is not all miracles, but they do happen, too, and practically anywhere. Perhaps also on these pages, here in this book. If you cannot see this, picture it and take a plunge.

At the end of a faded day, I land on an imitation leather sofa in
a clinical office room, like a leaf falling from a tree. I am cooked
in the stuffy air. Markku and I are trying to get into the swing of
things, planning a course for the coming spring and discussing issues
that some of the students are struggling with in their studies. We go
through the motions of wondering about the lack of money and time,
as we have all become accustomed to doing.

Epilogue

Markku
Hakuri

Epilogue

For a long time, the working title for this book was *12 Years That Changed the World* – environmental art playing the role of reformer. However the grandiosity of the title seemed to overshadow the content. The original main topic was the union of place and space. This is a pair of concepts that puzzles makers of environmental art, and something that is continually being addressed in environmental art education.

The authors of the articles in the book are important people to me. They all have contributed to the contents of the degree programme in environmental art. Their original perspectives on environmental art, the concepts of place and space, and the contents of the education form the core of this book.

I have asked three authors, Jan-Erik Andersson, Daniel Snow and Kurt Vanbelleghem, to describe, from their own perspective, the hands-on instruction, including the workshop on environmental art that they taught. Other writers, Polly Balitro, Scott Elliott, Tristan Hamel, Martti Hyvönen, Ossi Naukkarinen, Laura Uimonen and Jan Kenneth Weckman, have chosen the form and perspective of their articles according to my brief, which was: a free hand to approach issues related to environmental art and its teaching.

I would like to thank all the writers, and each one separately, for their inspiring involvement, both as friends and colleagues. Their contribution truly is the core of this book. I would also like to thank Dean Helena Hyvönen, whose go-ahead gave this book a chance to come into existence. My thanks also go to the Aalto ARTS Books staff for their valuable support, and Helsingin Energia for finally enabling this book to be made. The biggest thank goes to my wife Kaarina, who, characteristically, spared no effort in pushing me forward, proofreading, transcribing, and, instead of just reading, critiquing the text.

INDEX OF PHOTOGRAPHS

PAIKKA

VAI

TILA